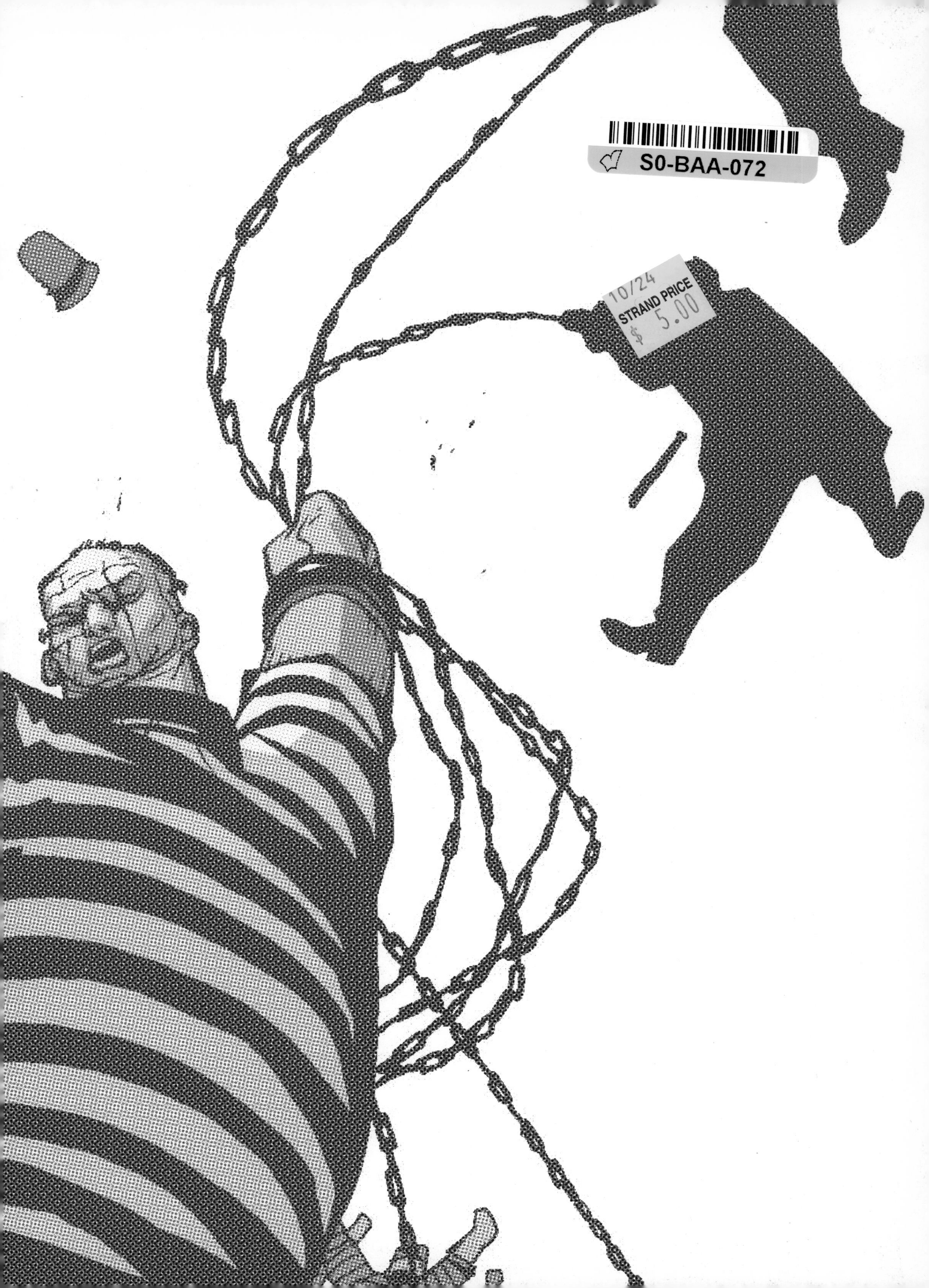

CARLOS TRILLO   JUAN BOBILLO

ZACHARY HOLMES

Case One: The Monster

Venture

DARK HORSE COMICS • STRIP ART FEATURES

Carlos Trillo • Juan Bobillo
ZACHARY HOLMES
Case One - The Monster

© Strip Art Features, 2001, www.safcomics.com
All rights reserved.

Published by
DARK HORSE COMICS, Inc.
10956 SE Main Street
Milwaukie, Oregon 97222, USA
www.darkhorse.com

First edition: November 2001
ISBN: 1-56971-702-8

Color separations: SAF - ScanArt, Slovenia
Printed in Slovenia by SAF - Tiskarna Koper

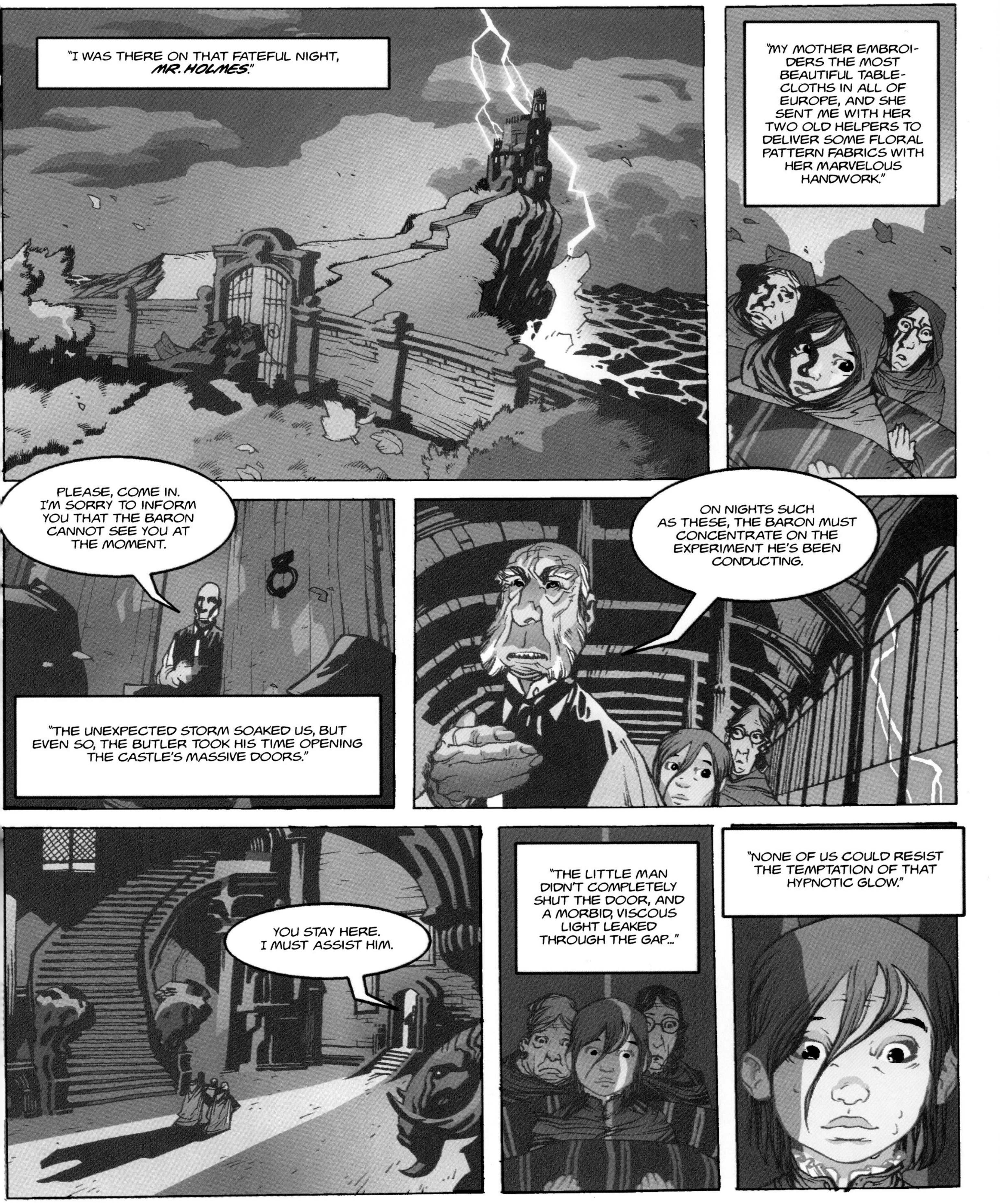
"I WAS THERE ON THAT FATEFUL NIGHT, ***MR. HOLMES***."
"MY MOTHER EMBROIDERS THE MOST BEAUTIFUL TABLECLOTHS IN ALL OF EUROPE, AND SHE SENT ME WITH HER TWO OLD HELPERS TO DELIVER SOME FLORAL PATTERN FABRICS WITH HER MARVELOUS HANDWORK."
PLEASE, COME IN. I'M SORRY TO INFORM YOU THAT THE BARON CANNOT SEE YOU AT THE MOMENT.
"THE UNEXPECTED STORM SOAKED US, BUT EVEN SO, THE BUTLER TOOK HIS TIME OPENING THE CASTLE'S MASSIVE DOORS."
ON NIGHTS SUCH AS THESE, THE BARON MUST CONCENTRATE ON THE EXPERIMENT HE'S BEEN CONDUCTING.
YOU STAY HERE. I MUST ASSIST HIM.
"THE LITTLE MAN DIDN'T COMPLETELY SHUT THE DOOR, AND A MORBID, VISCOUS LIGHT LEAKED THROUGH THE GAP..."
"NONE OF US COULD RESIST THE TEMPTATION OF THAT HYPNOTIC GLOW."

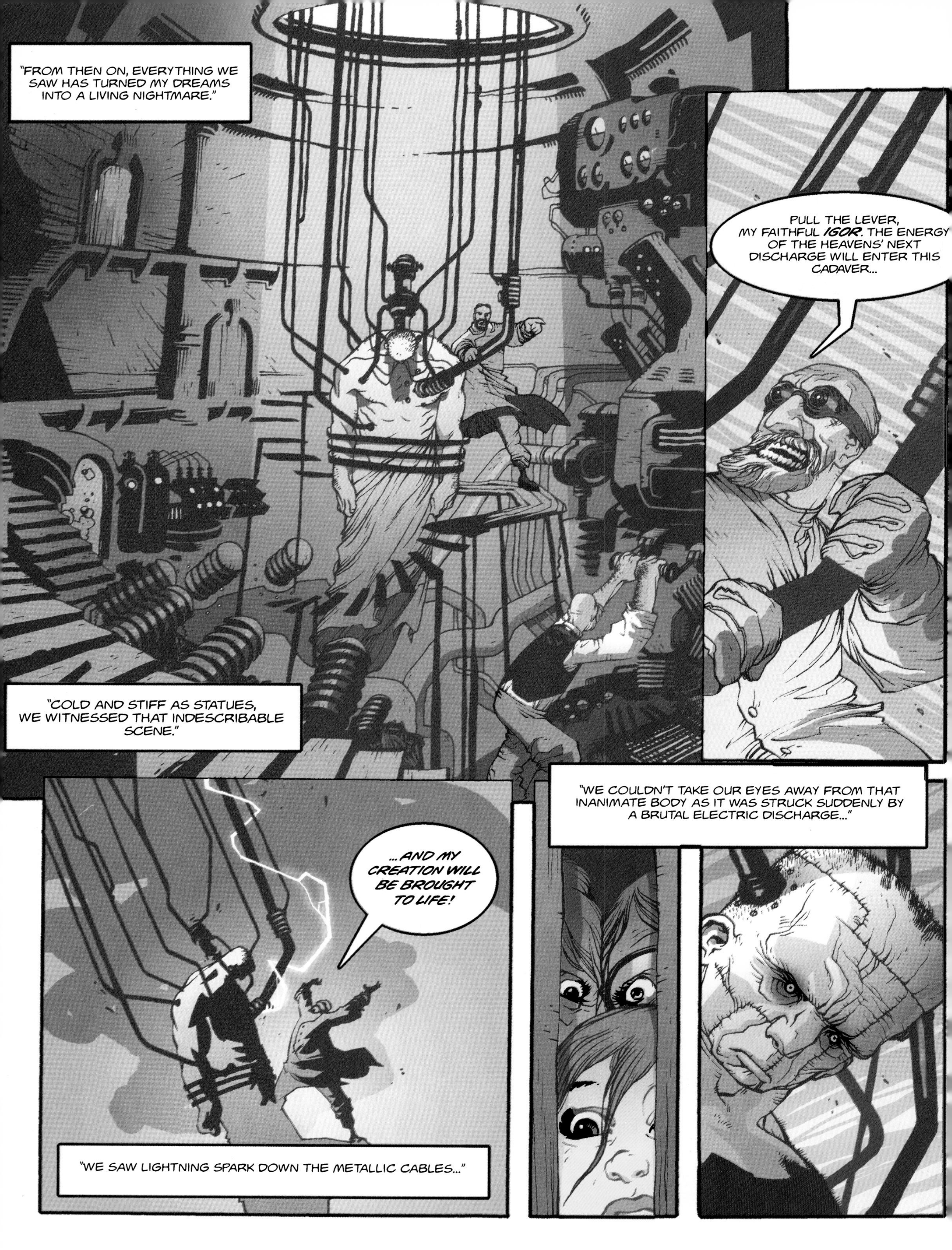
"FROM THEN ON, EVERYTHING WE SAW HAS TURNED MY DREAMS INTO A LIVING NIGHTMARE."
PULL THE LEVER, MY FAITHFUL IGOR. THE ENERGY OF THE HEAVENS' NEXT DISCHARGE WILL ENTER THIS CADAVER...
"COLD AND STIFF AS STATUES, WE WITNESSED THAT INDESCRIBABLE SCENE."
...AND MY CREATION WILL BE BROUGHT TO LIFE!
"WE SAW LIGHTNING SPARK DOWN THE METALLIC CABLES..."
"WE COULDN'T TAKE OUR EYES AWAY FROM THAT INANIMATE BODY AS IT WAS STRUCK SUDDENLY BY A BRUTAL ELECTRIC DISCHARGE..."

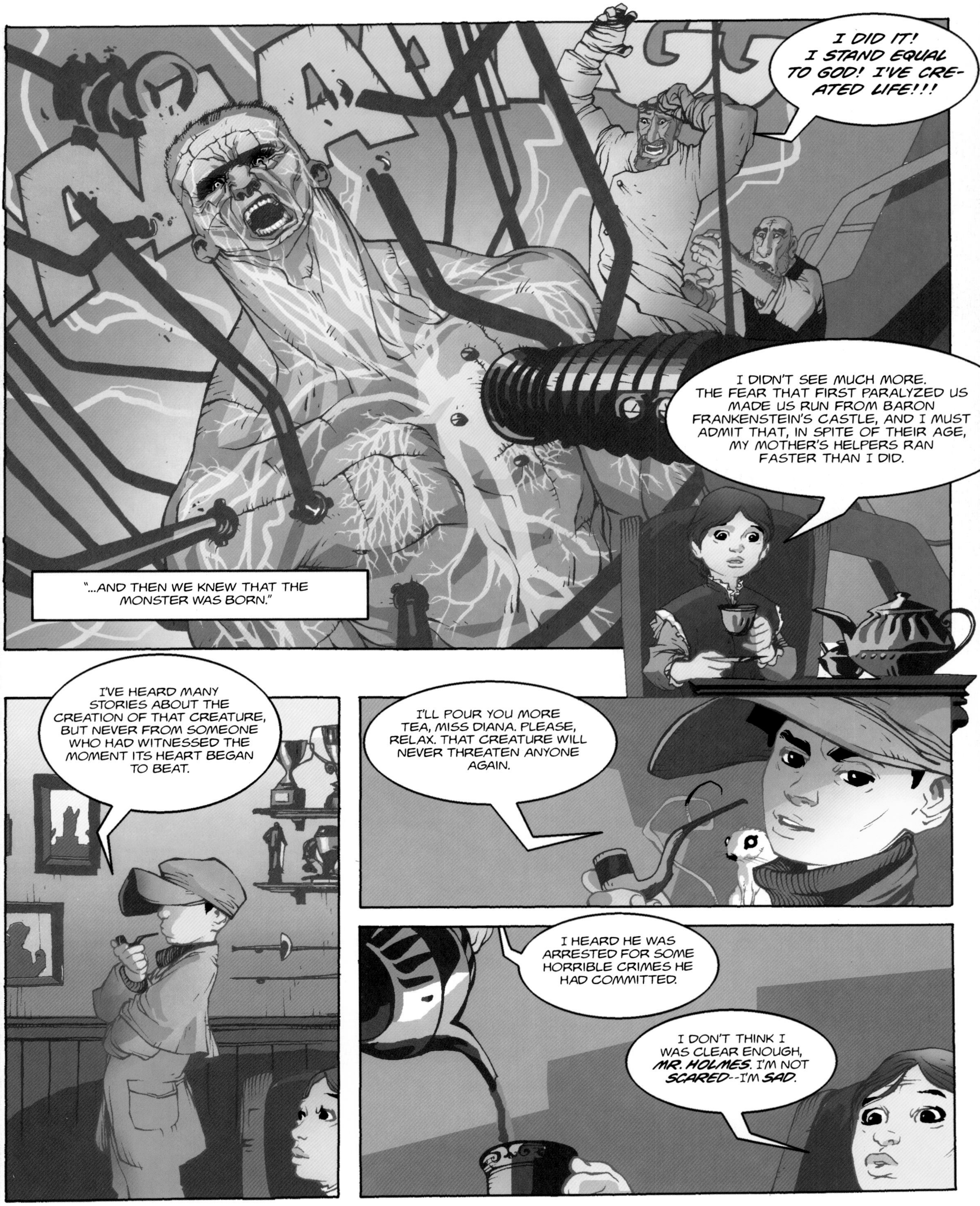
I DID IT! I STAND EQUAL TO GOD! I'VE CRE-ATED LIFE!!!
I DIDN'T SEE MUCH MORE. THE FEAR THAT FIRST PARALYZED US MADE US RUN FROM BARON FRANKENSTEIN'S CASTLE, AND I MUST ADMIT THAT, IN SPITE OF THEIR AGE, MY MOTHER'S HELPERS RAN FASTER THAN I DID.
"...AND THEN WE KNEW THAT THE MONSTER WAS BORN."
I'VE HEARD MANY STORIES ABOUT THE CREATION OF THAT CREATURE, BUT NEVER FROM SOMEONE WHO HAD WITNESSED THE MOMENT ITS HEART BEGAN TO BEAT.
I'LL POUR YOU MORE TEA, MISS DIANA. PLEASE, RELAX. THAT CREATURE WILL NEVER THREATEN ANYONE AGAIN.
I HEARD HE WAS ARRESTED FOR SOME HORRIBLE CRIMES HE HAD COMMITTED.
I DON'T THINK I WAS CLEAR ENOUGH, MR. HOLMES. I'M NOT SCARED--I'M SAD.

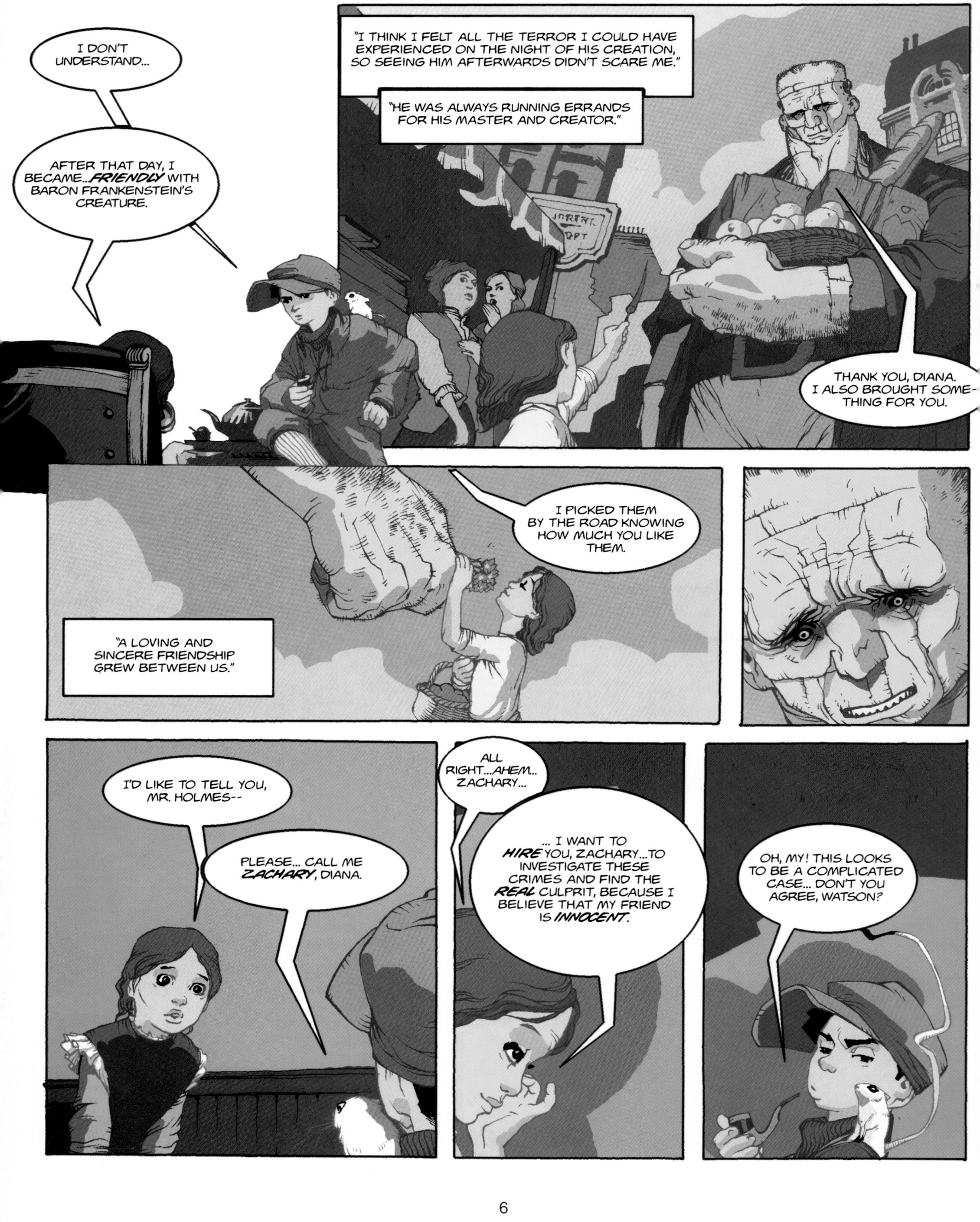
I DON'T UNDERSTAND...
AFTER THAT DAY, I BECAME...FRIENDLY WITH BARON FRANKENSTEIN'S CREATURE.
"I THINK I FELT ALL THE TERROR I COULD HAVE EXPERIENCED ON THE NIGHT OF HIS CREATION, SO SEEING HIM AFTERWARDS DIDN'T SCARE ME."
"HE WAS ALWAYS RUNNING ERRANDS FOR HIS MASTER AND CREATOR."
THANK YOU, DIANA. I ALSO BROUGHT SOMETHING FOR YOU.
I PICKED THEM BY THE ROAD KNOWING HOW MUCH YOU LIKE THEM.
"A LOVING AND SINCERE FRIENDSHIP GREW BETWEEN US."
I'D LIKE TO TELL YOU, MR. HOLMES--
PLEASE... CALL ME ZACHARY, DIANA.
ALL RIGHT...AHEM.. ZACHARY...
... I WANT TO HIRE YOU, ZACHARY...TO INVESTIGATE THESE CRIMES AND FIND THE REAL CULPRIT, BECAUSE I BELIEVE THAT MY FRIEND IS INNOCENT.
OH, MY! THIS LOOKS TO BE A COMPLICATED CASE... DON'T YOU AGREE, WATSON?

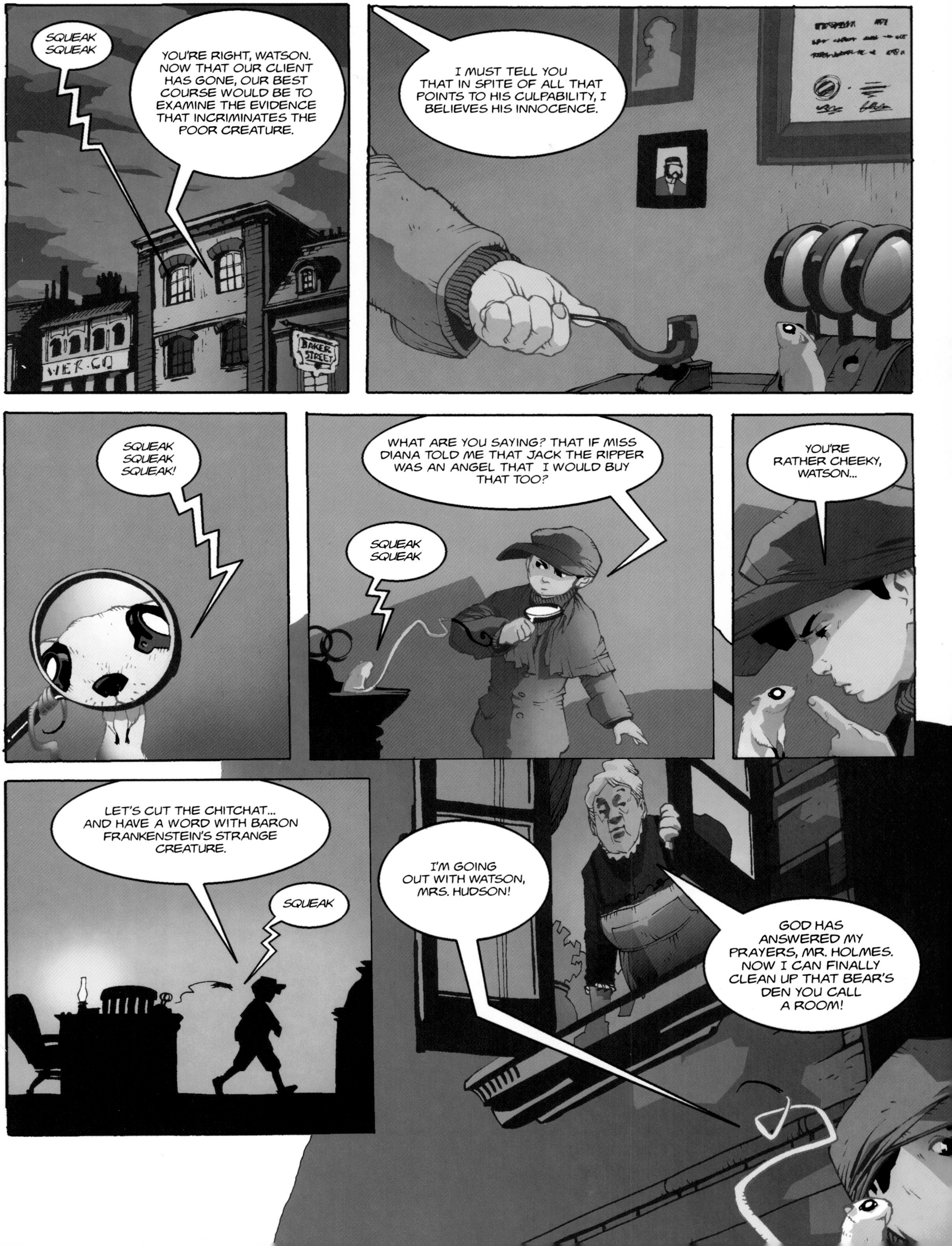
SQUEAK SQUEAK
YOU'RE RIGHT, WATSON. NOW THAT OUR CLIENT HAS GONE, OUR BEST COURSE WOULD BE TO EXAMINE THE EVIDENCE THAT INCRIMINATES THE POOR CREATURE.
WIER-CO
BAKER STREET
I MUST TELL YOU THAT IN SPITE OF ALL THAT POINTS TO HIS CULPABILITY, I BELIEVES HIS INNOCENCE.
SQUEAK SQUEAK SQUEAK!
WHAT ARE YOU SAYING? THAT IF MISS DIANA TOLD ME THAT JACK THE RIPPER WAS AN ANGEL THAT I WOULD BUY THAT TOO?
SQUEAK SQUEAK
YOU'RE RATHER CHEEKY, WATSON...
LET'S CUT THE CHITCHAT... AND HAVE A WORD WITH BARON FRANKENSTEIN'S STRANGE CREATURE.
SQUEAK
I'M GOING OUT WITH WATSON, MRS. HUDSON!
GOD HAS ANSWERED MY PRAYERS, MR. HOLMES. NOW I CAN FINALLY CLEAN UP THAT BEAR'S DEN YOU CALL A ROOM!

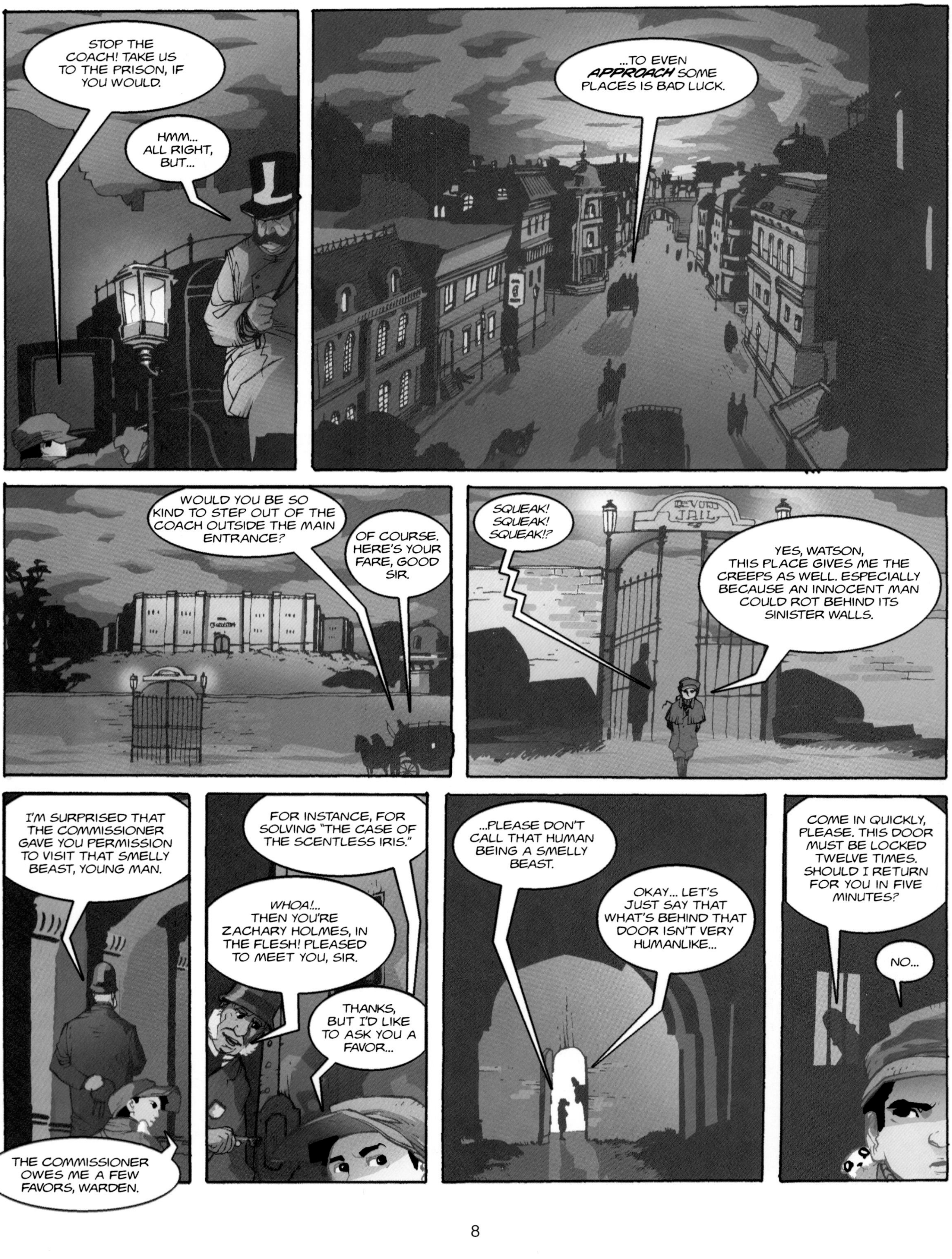
STOP THE COACH! TAKE US TO THE PRISON, IF YOU WOULD.
HMM... ALL RIGHT, BUT...
...TO EVEN APPROACH SOME PLACES IS BAD LUCK.
WOULD YOU BE SO KIND TO STEP OUT OF THE COACH OUTSIDE THE MAIN ENTRANCE?
OF COURSE. HERE'S YOUR FARE, GOOD SIR.
SQUEAK! SQUEAK! SQUEAK!?
JAIL
YES, WATSON, THIS PLACE GIVES ME THE CREEPS AS WELL. ESPECIALLY BECAUSE AN INNOCENT MAN COULD ROT BEHIND ITS SINISTER WALLS.
I'M SURPRISED THAT THE COMMISSIONER GAVE YOU PERMISSION TO VISIT THAT SMELLY BEAST, YOUNG MAN.
THE COMMISSIONER OWES ME A FEW FAVORS, WARDEN.
FOR INSTANCE, FOR SOLVING "THE CASE OF THE SCENTLESS IRIS."
WHOA!... THEN YOU'RE ZACHARY HOLMES, IN THE FLESH! PLEASED TO MEET YOU, SIR.
THANKS, BUT I'D LIKE TO ASK YOU A FAVOR...
...PLEASE DON'T CALL THAT HUMAN BEING A SMELLY BEAST.
OKAY... LET'S JUST SAY THAT WHAT'S BEHIND THAT DOOR ISN'T VERY HUMANLIKE...
COME IN QUICKLY, PLEASE. THIS DOOR MUST BE LOCKED TWELVE TIMES. SHOULD I RETURN FOR YOU IN FIVE MINUTES?
NO...

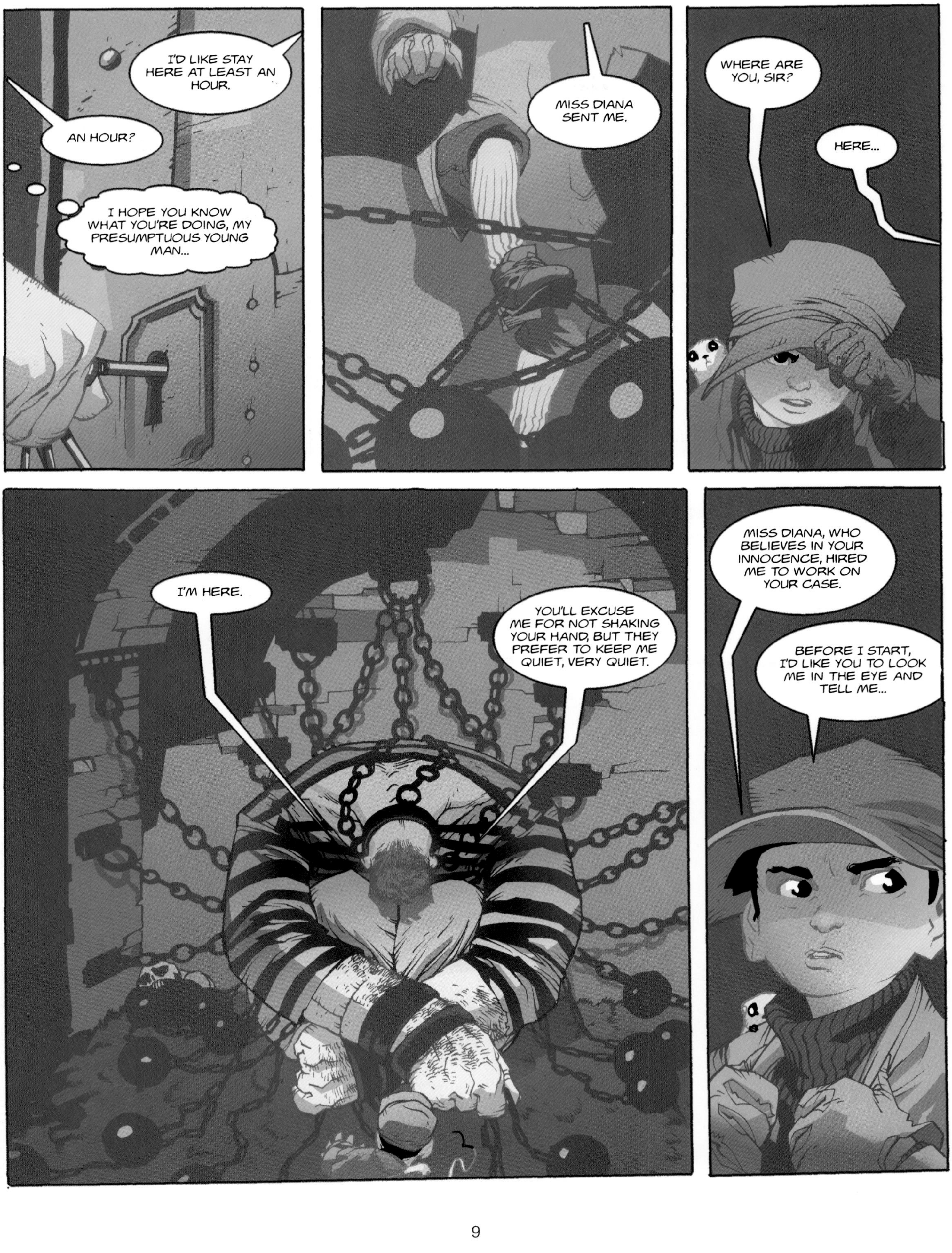
I'D LIKE STAY HERE AT LEAST AN HOUR.
AN HOUR?
I HOPE YOU KNOW WHAT YOU'RE DOING, MY PRESUMPTUOUS YOUNG MAN...
MISS DIANA SENT ME.
WHERE ARE YOU, SIR?
HERE...
I'M HERE.
YOU'LL EXCUSE ME FOR NOT SHAKING YOUR HAND, BUT THEY PREFER TO KEEP ME QUIET, VERY QUIET.
MISS DIANA, WHO BELIEVES IN YOUR INNOCENCE, HIRED ME TO WORK ON YOUR CASE.
BEFORE I START, I'D LIKE YOU TO LOOK ME IN THE EYE AND TELL ME...

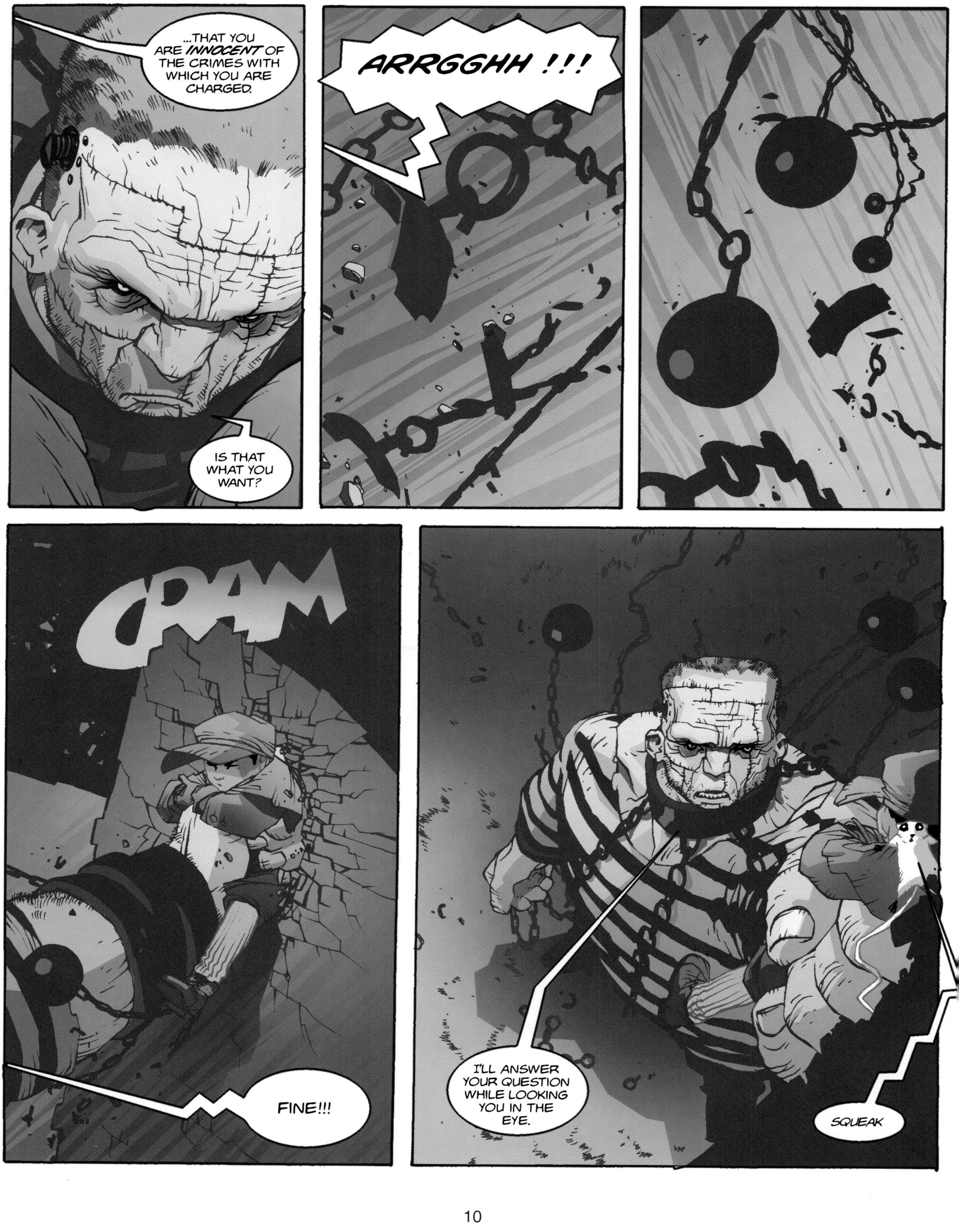
...THAT YOU ARE INNOCENT OF THE CRIMES WITH WHICH YOU ARE CHARGED.
IS THAT WHAT YOU WANT?
ARRGGHH !!!
CRAM
FINE!!!
I'LL ANSWER YOUR QUESTION WHILE LOOKING YOU IN THE EYE.
SQUEAK

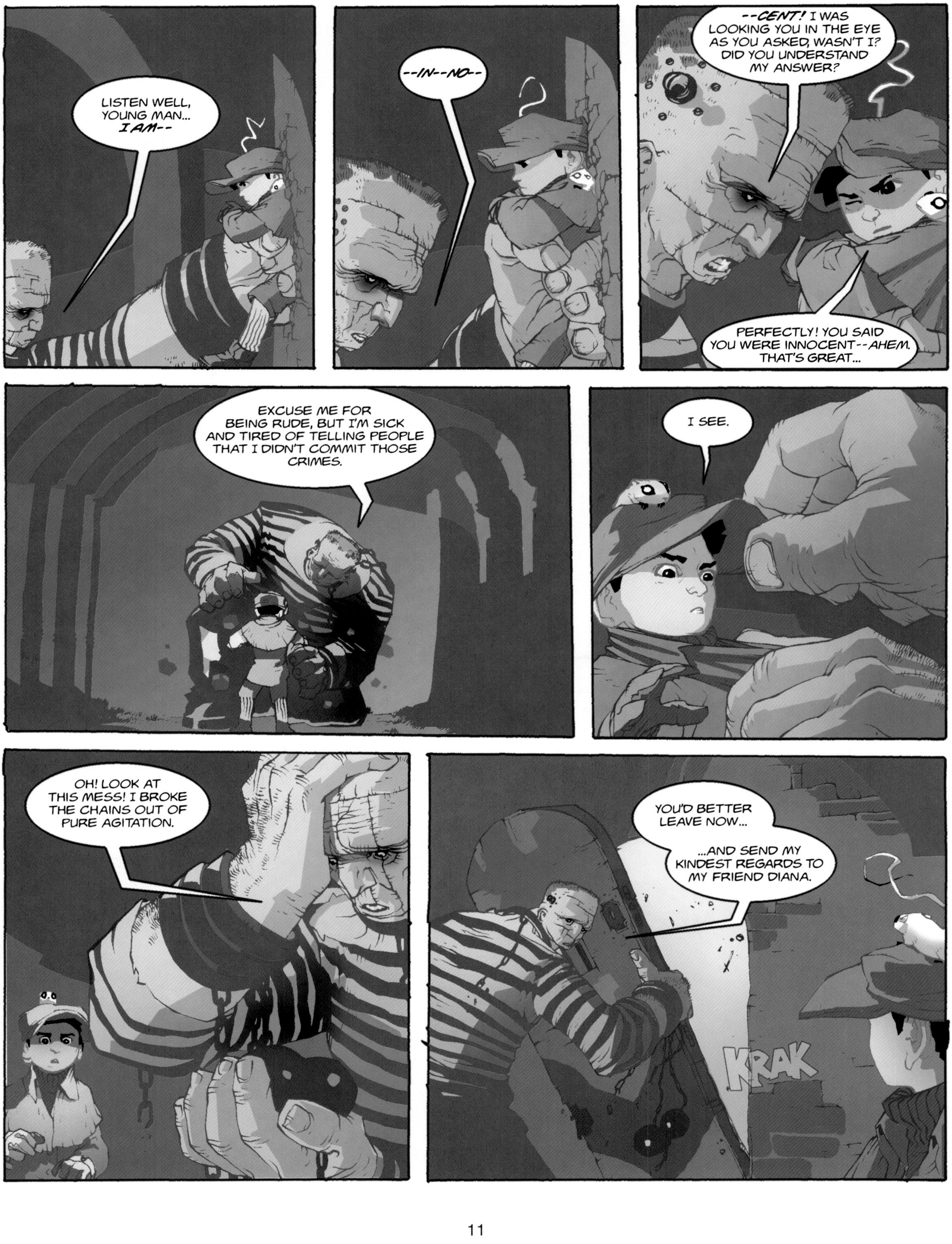
LISTEN WELL, YOUNG MAN... I AM--
--IN--NO--
--CENT! I WAS LOOKING YOU IN THE EYE AS YOU ASKED, WASN'T I? DID YOU UNDERSTAND MY ANSWER?
PERFECTLY! YOU SAID YOU WERE INNOCENT--AHEM. THAT'S GREAT...
EXCUSE ME FOR BEING RUDE, BUT I'M SICK AND TIRED OF TELLING PEOPLE THAT I DIDN'T COMMIT THOSE CRIMES.
I SEE.
OH! LOOK AT THIS MESS! I BROKE THE CHAINS OUT OF PURE AGITATION.
YOU'D BETTER LEAVE NOW...
...AND SEND MY KINDEST REGARDS TO MY FRIEND DIANA.
KRAK

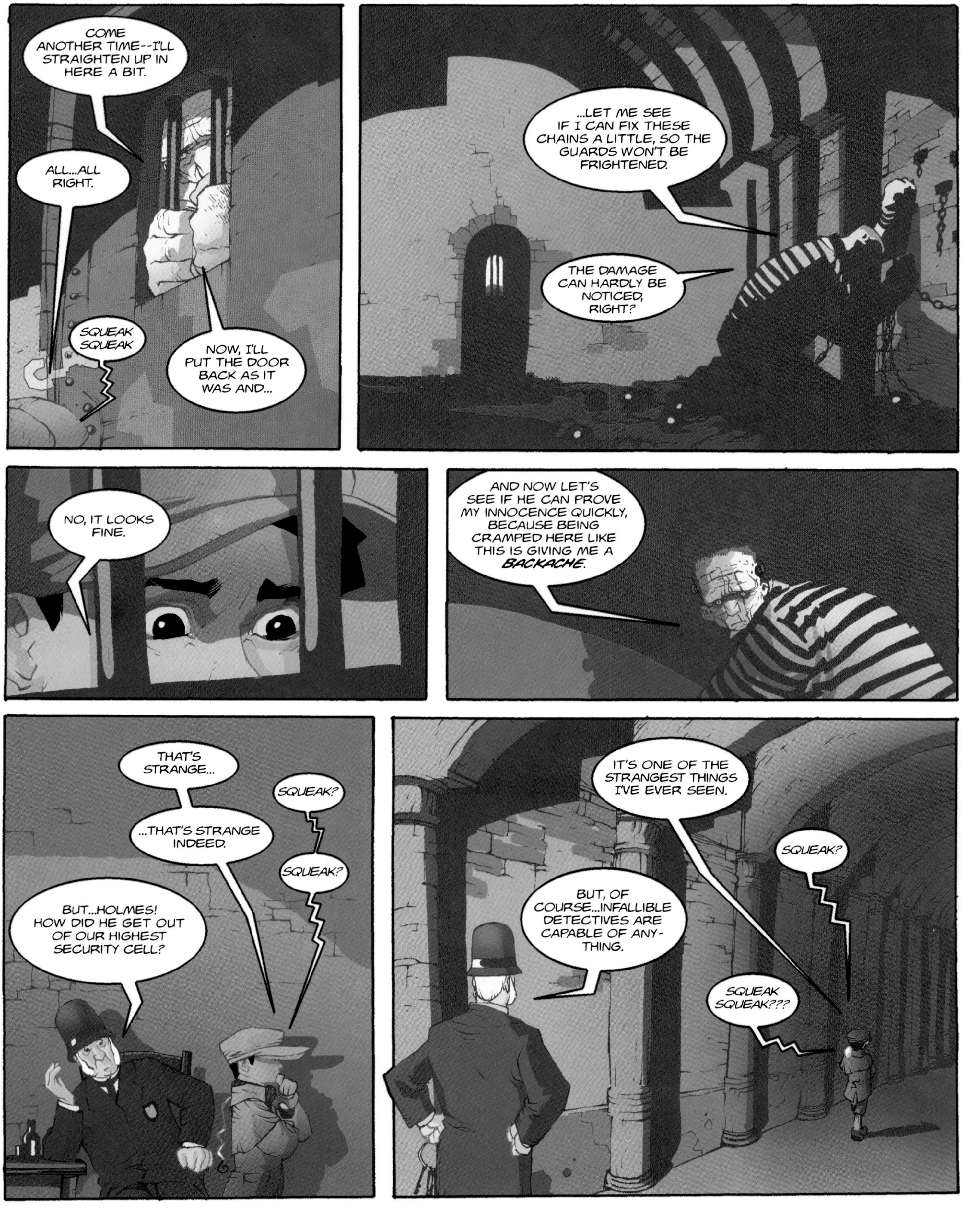
COME ANOTHER TIME--I'LL STRAIGHTEN UP IN HERE A BIT.
ALL...ALL RIGHT.
SQUEAK SQUEAK
NOW, I'LL PUT THE DOOR BACK AS IT WAS AND...
...LET ME SEE IF I CAN FIX THESE CHAINS A LITTLE, SO THE GUARDS WON'T BE FRIGHTENED.
THE DAMAGE CAN HARDLY BE NOTICED, RIGHT?
NO, IT LOOKS FINE.
AND NOW LET'S SEE IF HE CAN PROVE MY INNOCENCE QUICKLY, BECAUSE BEING CRAMPED HERE LIKE THIS IS GIVING ME A *BACKACHE*.
THAT'S STRANGE...
...THAT'S STRANGE INDEED.
SQUEAK?
SQUEAK?
BUT...HOLMES! HOW DID HE GET OUT OF OUR HIGHEST SECURITY CELL?
IT'S ONE OF THE STRANGEST THINGS I'VE EVER SEEN.
SQUEAK?
BUT, OF COURSE...INFALLIBLE DETECTIVES ARE CAPABLE OF ANY-THING.
SQUEAK SQUEAK???

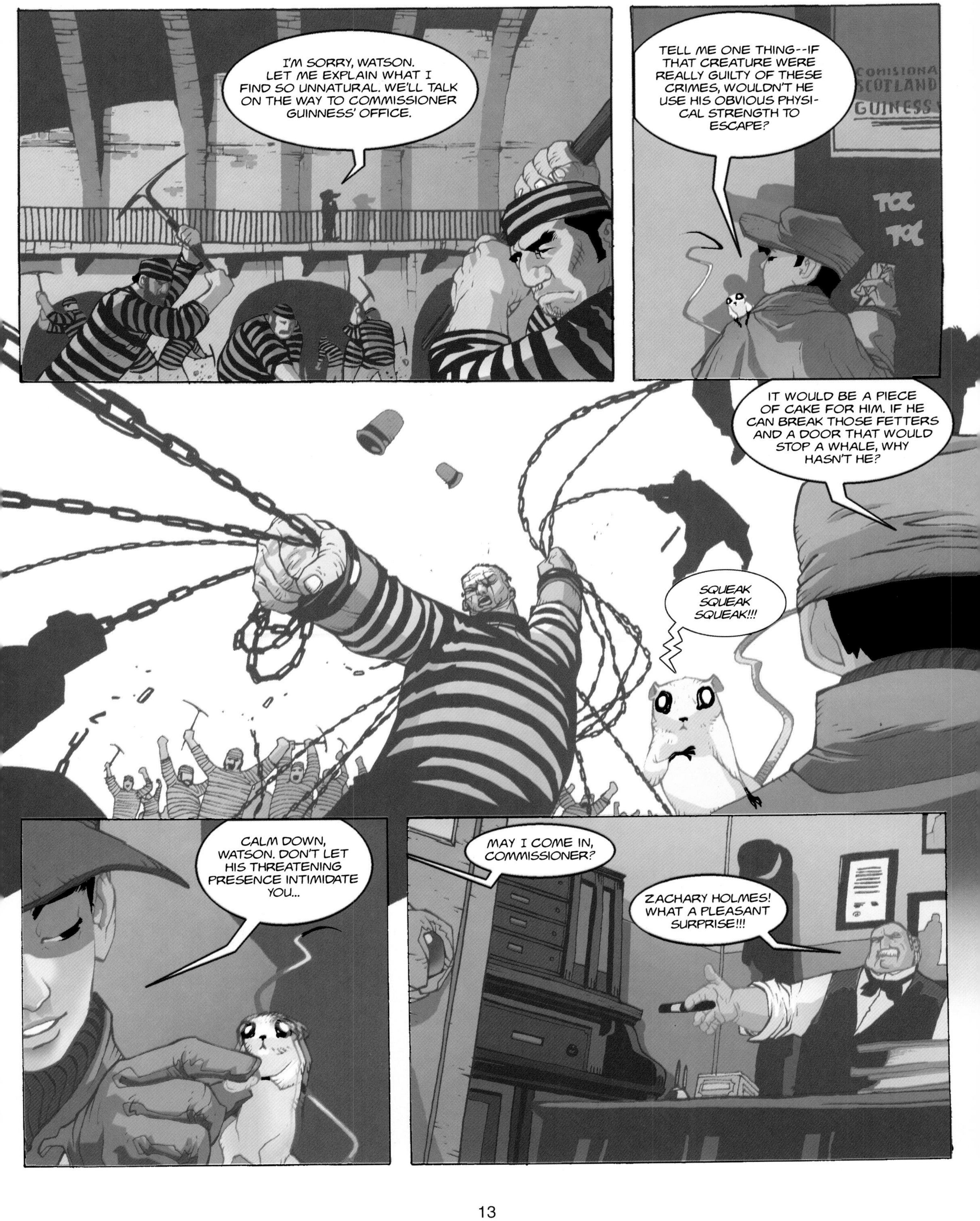
I'M SORRY, WATSON. LET ME EXPLAIN WHAT I FIND SO UNNATURAL. WE'LL TALK ON THE WAY TO COMMISSIONER GUINNESS' OFFICE.
TELL ME ONE THING--IF THAT CREATURE WERE REALLY GUILTY OF THESE CRIMES, WOULDN'T HE USE HIS OBVIOUS PHYSI-CAL STRENGTH TO ESCAPE?
COMISIONA
SCOTLAND
GUINESS
TOC
TOC
IT WOULD BE A PIECE OF CAKE FOR HIM. IF HE CAN BREAK THOSE FETTERS AND A DOOR THAT WOULD STOP A WHALE, WHY HASN'T HE?
SQUEAK SQUEAK SQUEAK!!!
CALM DOWN, WATSON. DON'T LET HIS THREATENING PRESENCE INTIMIDATE YOU...
MAY I COME IN, COMMISSIONER?
ZACHARY HOLMES! WHAT A PLEASANT SURPRISE!!!

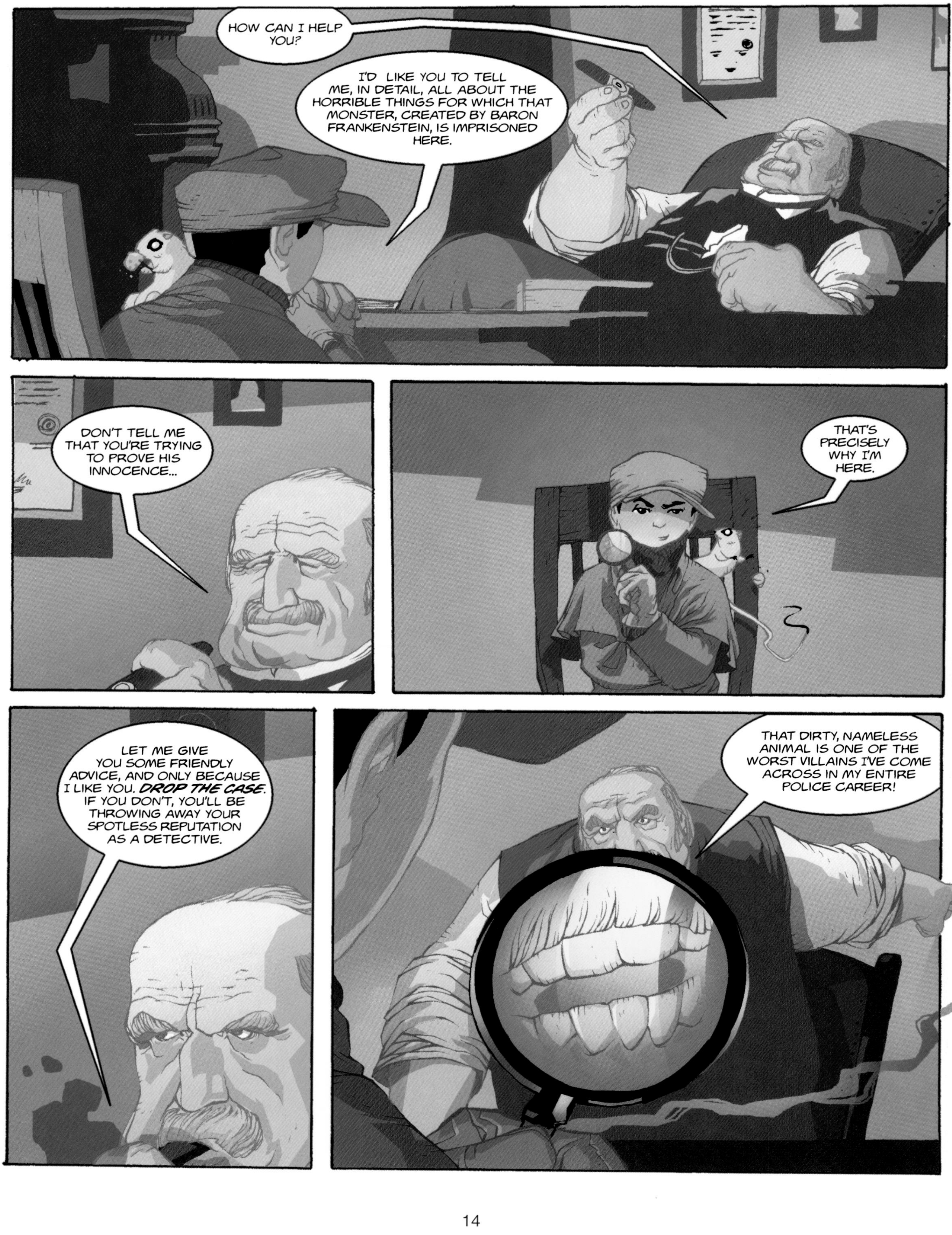
HOW CAN I HELP YOU?
I'D LIKE YOU TO TELL ME, IN DETAIL, ALL ABOUT THE HORRIBLE THINGS FOR WHICH THAT MONSTER, CREATED BY BARON FRANKENSTEIN, IS IMPRISONED HERE.
DON'T TELL ME THAT YOU'RE TRYING TO PROVE HIS INNOCENCE...
THAT'S PRECISELY WHY I'M HERE.
LET ME GIVE YOU SOME FRIENDLY ADVICE, AND ONLY BECAUSE I LIKE YOU. ***DROP THE CASE***. IF YOU DON'T, YOU'LL BE THROWING AWAY YOUR SPOTLESS REPUTATION AS A DETECTIVE.
THAT DIRTY, NAMELESS ANIMAL IS ONE OF THE WORST VILLAINS I'VE COME ACROSS IN MY ENTIRE POLICE CAREER!

ARENʼT YOU EXAGGERATING A BIT, COMMISSIONER?

NOT AT ALL. UNFORTUNATELY, THE BARON WANTED TO PLAY GOD AND CREATE LIFE.

BESIDES, IʼM SURE THAT ONLY GODʼS PUNISHMENT COULD HAVE CREATED THAT PATHETIC PARODY OF MANKIND. HAVE YOU NOTICED WHATʼS MISSING IN THE CELL OF THAT UNSPEAKABLE BASTARD, ZACHARY?

RATS! DO YOU REALIZE THAT? NOT EVEN FILTHY RODENTS CAN STAND BEING AROUND HIM!

WHY DONʼT YOU TELL ME ABOUT THE CRIMES THAT FRANKENSTEINʼS CREATURE COMMITTED, ONE BY ONE? AND WATSON, PLEASE DONʼT DISTURB ME.

I WILL, IN CHRONOLOGICAL ORDER. FIRST, IN A SUDDEN FIT OF RAGE, HE DESTROYED HIS CREATORʼS HOME.

MY LORD! HEʼS BREAKING EVERY-THING! COME!

AAARGHHHH! IʼVE HATED THIS PLACE FROM THE DAY I WAS BORN!

STOP THIS INSTANT! HOW DARE YOU DESTROY THE PROPERTY OF HE WHO GAVE YOU LIFE?

LIFE?!

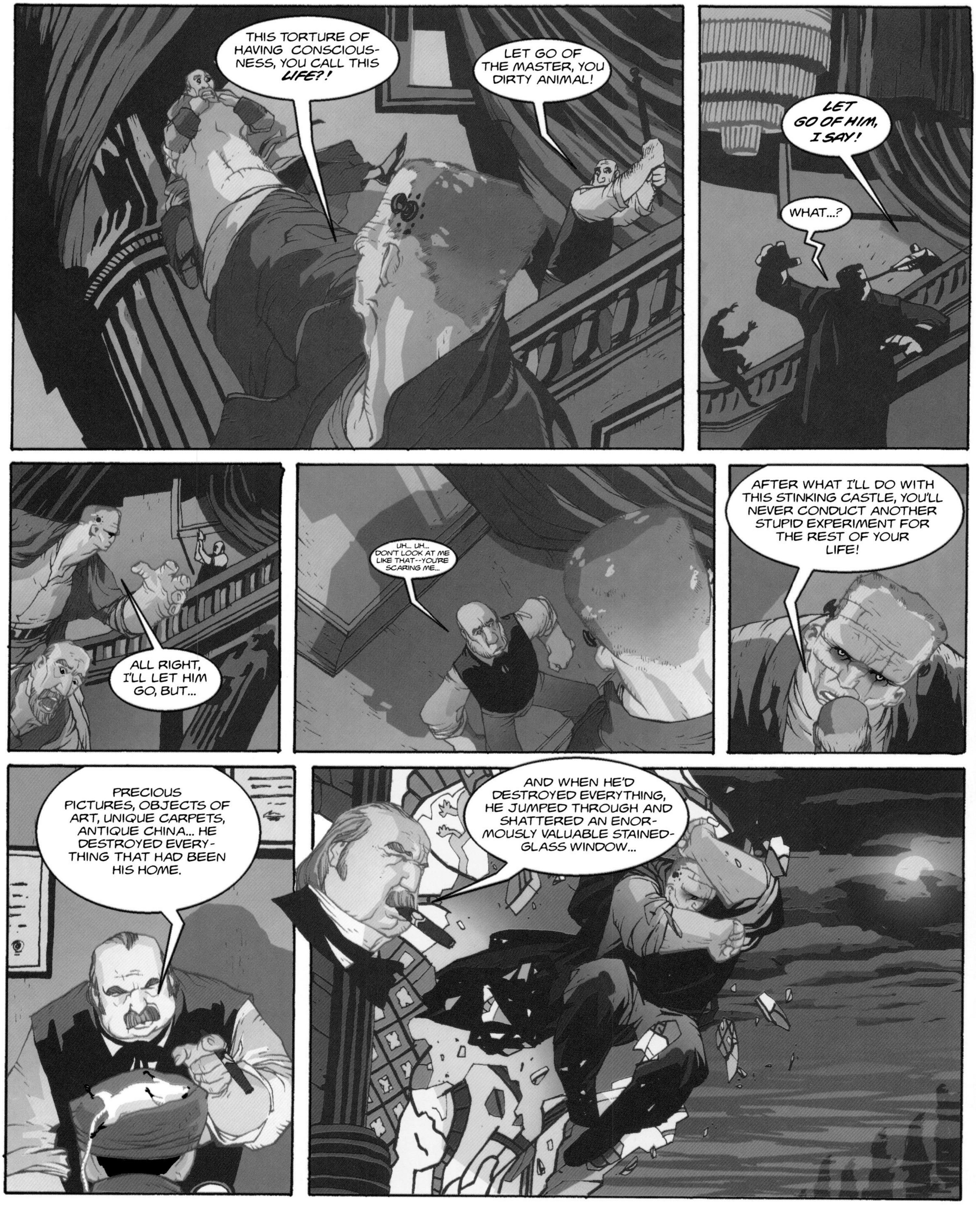
THIS TORTURE OF HAVING CONSCIOUSNESS, YOU CALL THIS LIFE?!
LET GO OF THE MASTER, YOU DIRTY ANIMAL!
LET GO OF HIM, I SAY!
WHAT...?
ALL RIGHT, I'LL LET HIM GO, BUT...
UH... UH... DON'T LOOK AT ME LIKE THAT--YOU'RE SCARING ME...
AFTER WHAT I'LL DO WITH THIS STINKING CASTLE, YOU'LL NEVER CONDUCT ANOTHER STUPID EXPERIMENT FOR THE REST OF YOUR LIFE!
PRECIOUS PICTURES, OBJECTS OF ART, UNIQUE CARPETS, ANTIQUE CHINA... HE DESTROYED EVERYTHING THAT HAD BEEN HIS HOME.
AND WHEN HE'D DESTROYED EVERYTHING, HE JUMPED THROUGH AND SHATTERED AN ENORMOUSLY VALUABLE STAINED-GLASS WINDOW...

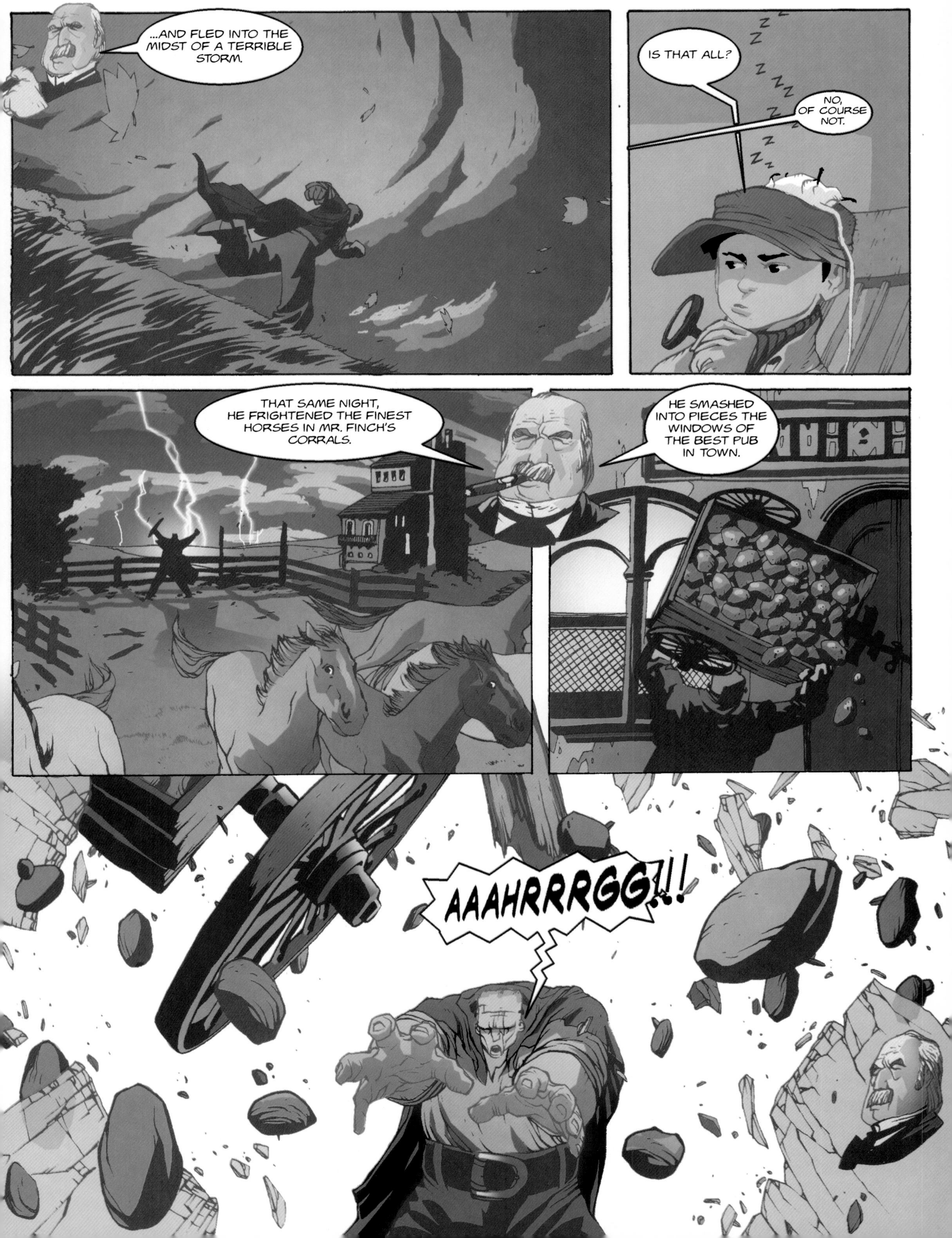
...AND FLED INTO THE MIDST OF A TERRIBLE STORM.
IS THAT ALL?
NO, OF COURSE NOT.
THAT SAME NIGHT, HE FRIGHTENED THE FINEST HORSES IN MR. FINCH'S CORRALS.
HE SMASHED INTO PIECES THE WINDOWS OF THE BEST PUB IN TOWN.
AAAHRRRGG!!!

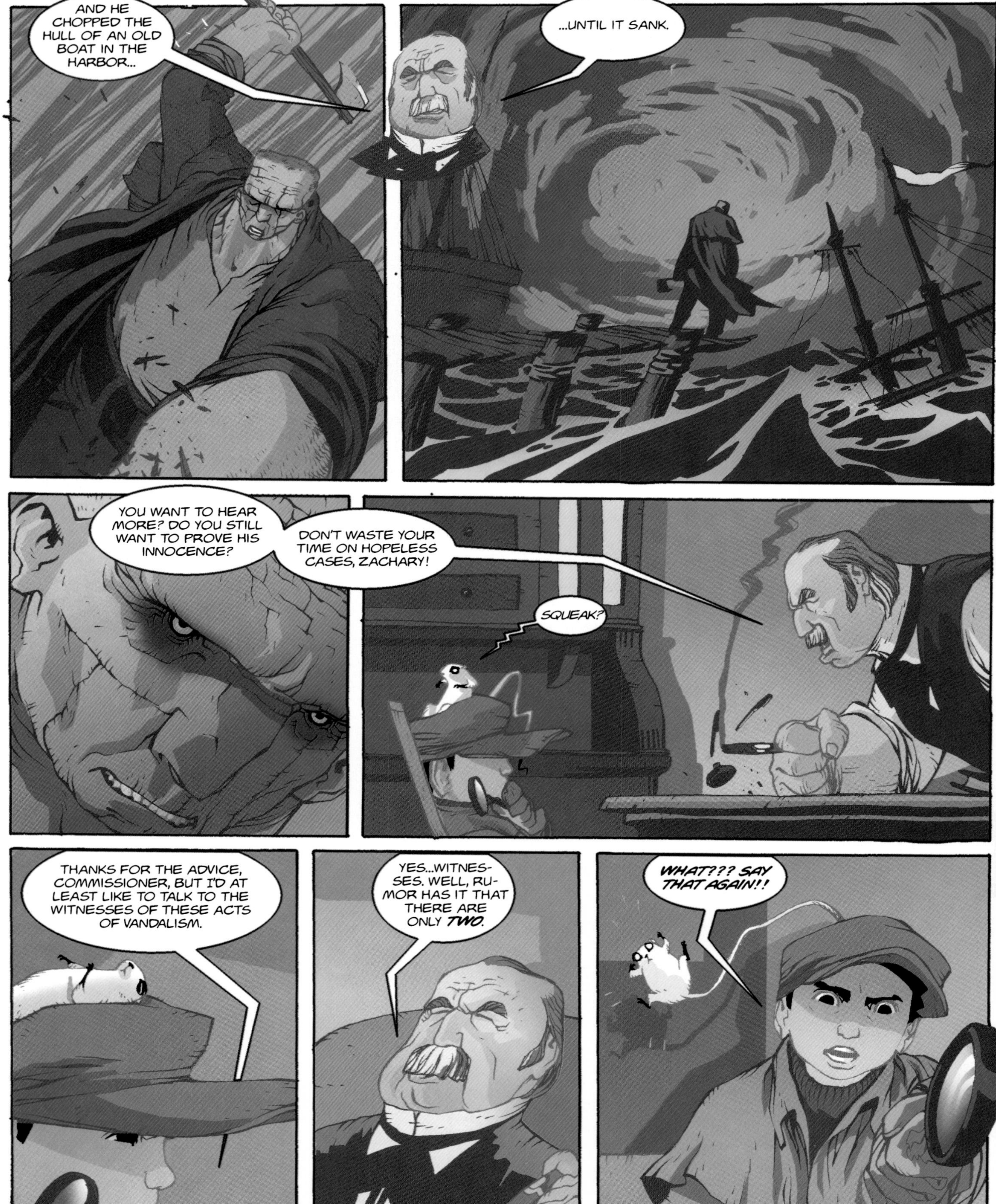
AND HE CHOPPED THE HULL OF AN OLD BOAT IN THE HARBOR...
...UNTIL IT SANK.
YOU WANT TO HEAR MORE? DO YOU STILL WANT TO PROVE HIS INNOCENCE?
DON'T WASTE YOUR TIME ON HOPELESS CASES, ZACHARY!
SQUEAK?
THANKS FOR THE ADVICE, COMMISSIONER, BUT I'D AT LEAST LIKE TO TALK TO THE WITNESSES OF THESE ACTS OF VANDALISM.
YES...WITNESSES. WELL, RUMOR HAS IT THAT THERE ARE ONLY TWO.
WHAT??? SAY THAT AGAIN!!

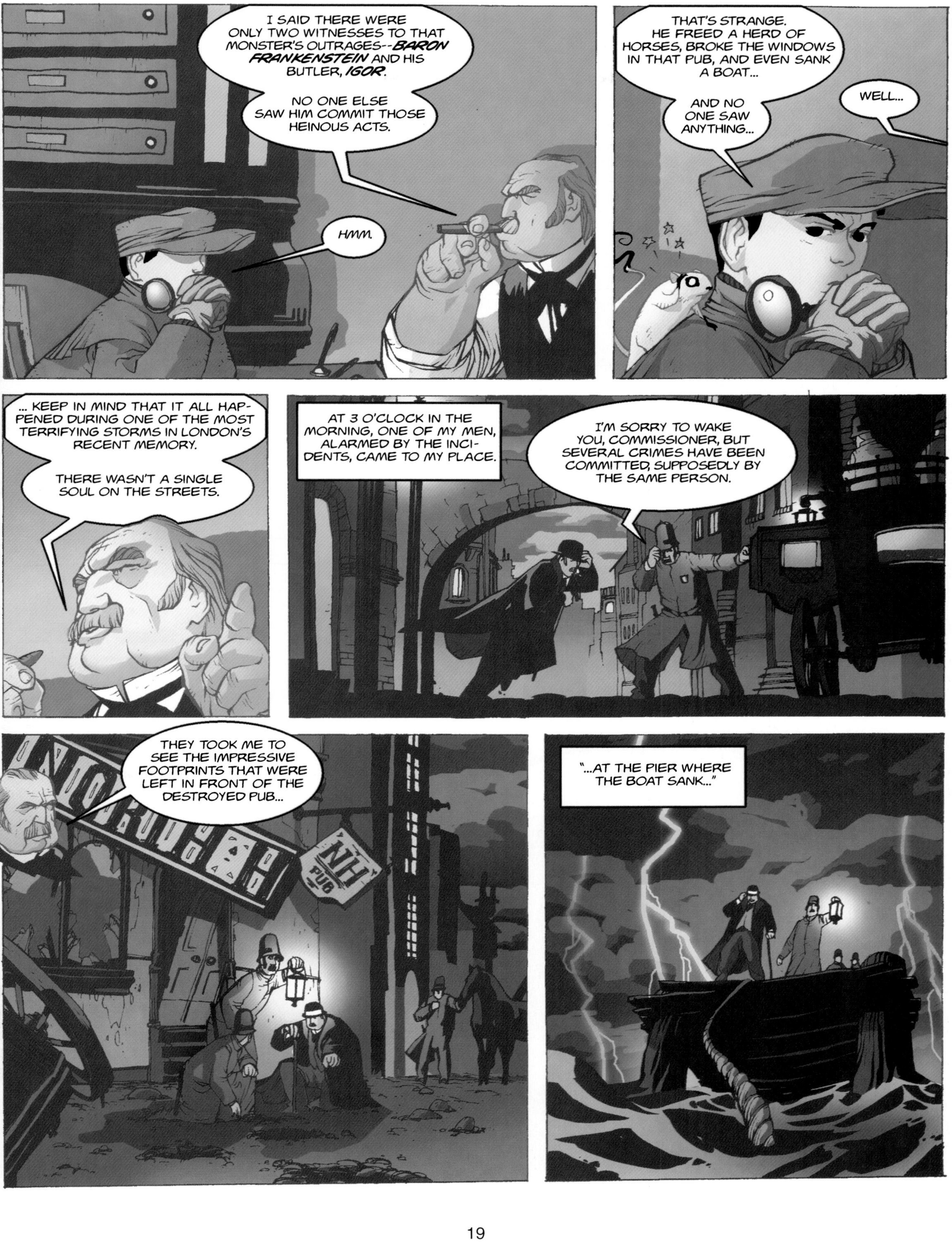

I SAID THERE WERE ONLY TWO WITNESSES TO THAT MONSTER'S OUTRAGES--BARON FRANKENSTEIN AND HIS BUTLER, IGOR.
NO ONE ELSE SAW HIM COMMIT THOSE HEINOUS ACTS.
HMM.
THAT'S STRANGE. HE FREED A HERD OF HORSES, BROKE THE WINDOWS IN THAT PUB, AND EVEN SANK A BOAT...
AND NO ONE SAW ANYTHING...
WELL...
... KEEP IN MIND THAT IT ALL HAPPENED DURING ONE OF THE MOST TERRIFYING STORMS IN LONDON'S RECENT MEMORY.
THERE WASN'T A SINGLE SOUL ON THE STREETS.
AT 3 O'CLOCK IN THE MORNING, ONE OF MY MEN, ALARMED BY THE INCIDENTS, CAME TO MY PLACE.
I'M SORRY TO WAKE YOU, COMMISSIONER, BUT SEVERAL CRIMES HAVE BEEN COMMITTED, SUPPOSEDLY BY THE SAME PERSON.
THEY TOOK ME TO SEE THE IMPRESSIVE FOOTPRINTS THAT WERE LEFT IN FRONT OF THE DESTROYED PUB...
NH
PUB
"...AT THE PIER WHERE THE BOAT SANK..."

... AND IN MR. FINCH'S CORRALS.

NO HUMAN COULD HAVE LEFT FOOTPRINTS OF THAT SIZE.

WE THEN DECIDED TO GO TO BARON FRANKENSTEIN'S CASTLE...

... ALL THE EVIDENCE POINTED TO THE RESULT OF HIS MYSTERIOUS EXPERIMENT.

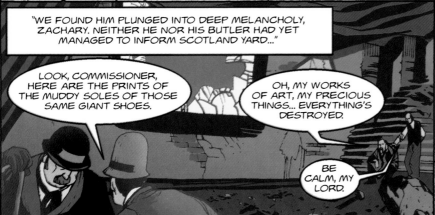

"WE FOUND HIM PLUNGED INTO DEEP MELANCHOLY, ZACHARY. NEITHER HE NOR HIS BUTLER HAD YET MANAGED TO INFORM SCOTLAND YARD..."

LOOK, COMMISSIONER, HERE ARE THE PRINTS OF THE MUDDY SOLES OF THOSE SAME GIANT SHOES.

OH, MY WORKS OF ART, MY PRECIOUS THINGS... EVERYTHING'S DESTROYED.

BE CALM, MY LORD.

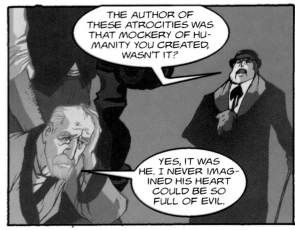

THE AUTHOR OF THESE ATROCITIES WAS THAT MOCKERY OF HUMANITY YOU CREATED, WASN'T IT?

YES, IT WAS HE. I NEVER IMAGINED HIS HEART COULD BE SO FULL OF EVIL.

MY MEN WENT TO SEARCH FOR THAT FREAK.

FINALLY, BEFORE THE STORM WAS OVER...

"...THEY FOUND HIM IN MRS. LONGER'S STABLE."

SURRENDER, SCOUNDREL! YOU'LL PAY FOR YOUR MALICE!

I DIDN'T DO ANYTHING!!

I'M AS INNOCENT AS A LAMB!!

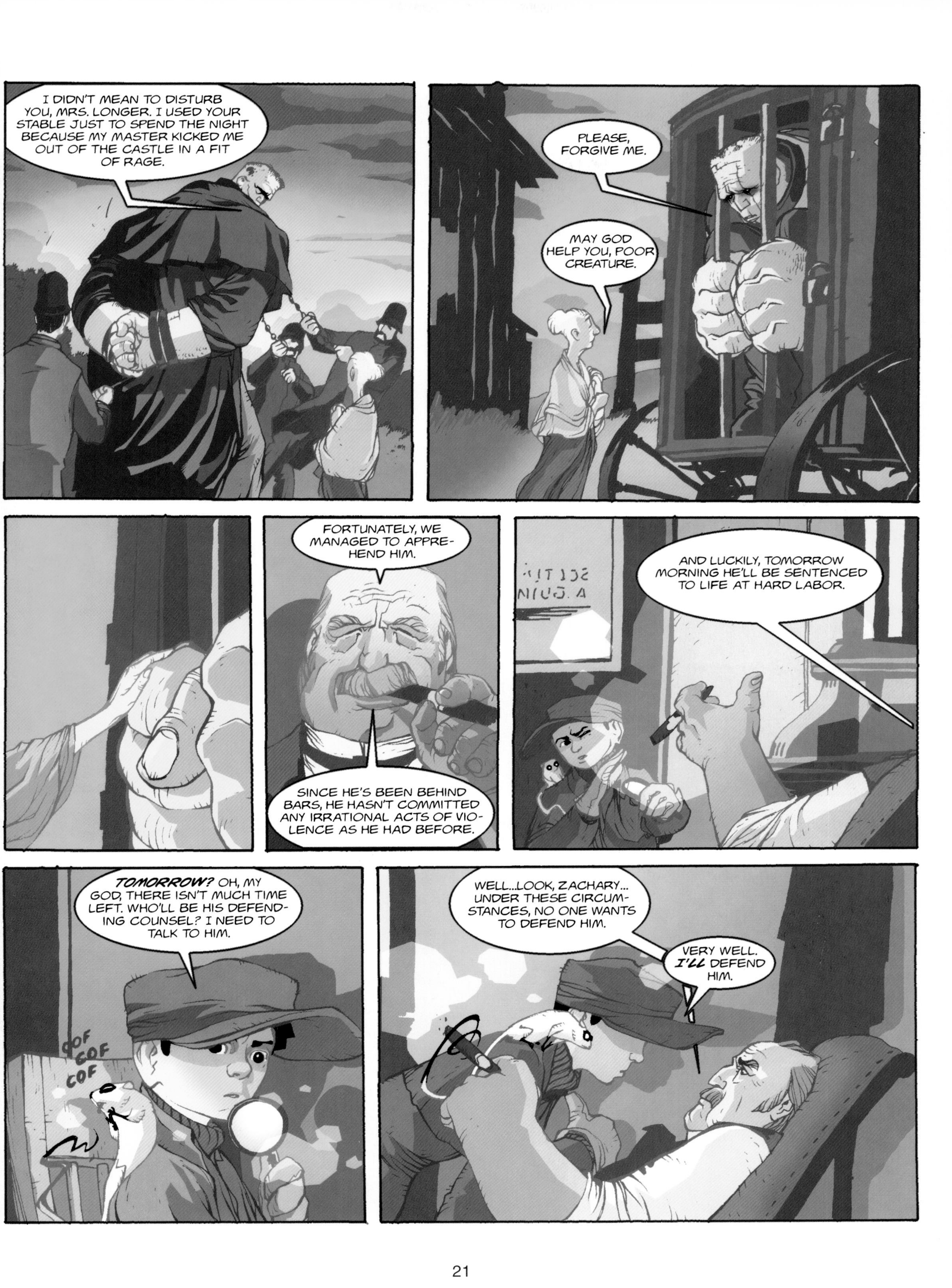
I DIDN'T MEAN TO DISTURB YOU, MRS. LONGER. I USED YOUR STABLE JUST TO SPEND THE NIGHT BECAUSE MY MASTER KICKED ME OUT OF THE CASTLE IN A FIT OF RAGE.
PLEASE, FORGIVE ME.
MAY GOD HELP YOU, POOR CREATURE.
FORTUNATELY, WE MANAGED TO APPREHEND HIM.
SINCE HE'S BEEN BEHIND BARS, HE HASN'T COMMITTED ANY IRRATIONAL ACTS OF VIOLENCE AS HE HAD BEFORE.
AND LUCKILY, TOMORROW MORNING HE'LL BE SENTENCED TO LIFE AT HARD LABOR.
TOMORROW? OH, MY GOD, THERE ISN'T MUCH TIME LEFT. WHO'LL BE HIS DEFENDING COUNSEL? I NEED TO TALK TO HIM.
COF COF COF
WELL...LOOK, ZACHARY... UNDER THESE CIRCUMSTANCES, NO ONE WANTS TO DEFEND HIM.
VERY WELL. *I'LL* DEFEND HIM.

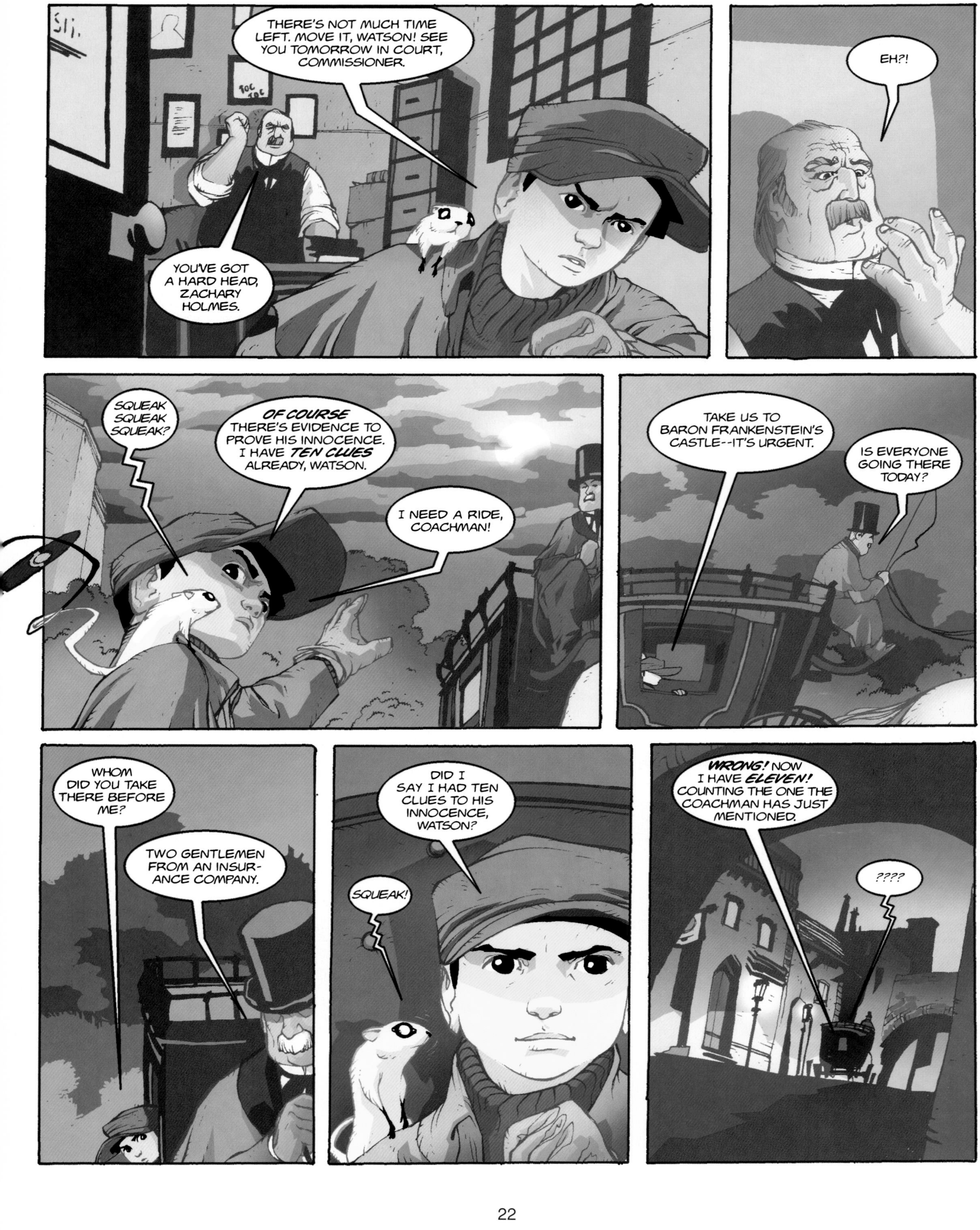
THERE'S NOT MUCH TIME LEFT. MOVE IT, WATSON! SEE YOU TOMORROW IN COURT, COMMISSIONER.
YOU'VE GOT A HARD HEAD, ZACHARY HOLMES.
EH?!
SQUEAK SQUEAK SQUEAK?
OF COURSE THERE'S EVIDENCE TO PROVE HIS INNOCENCE. I HAVE TEN CLUES ALREADY, WATSON.
I NEED A RIDE, COACHMAN!
TAKE US TO BARON FRANKENSTEIN'S CASTLE--IT'S URGENT.
IS EVERYONE GOING THERE TODAY?
WHOM DID YOU TAKE THERE BEFORE ME?
TWO GENTLEMEN FROM AN INSURANCE COMPANY.
DID I SAY I HAD TEN CLUES TO HIS INNOCENCE, WATSON?
SQUEAK!
WRONG! NOW I HAVE ELEVEN! COUNTING THE ONE THE COACHMAN HAS JUST MENTIONED.
????

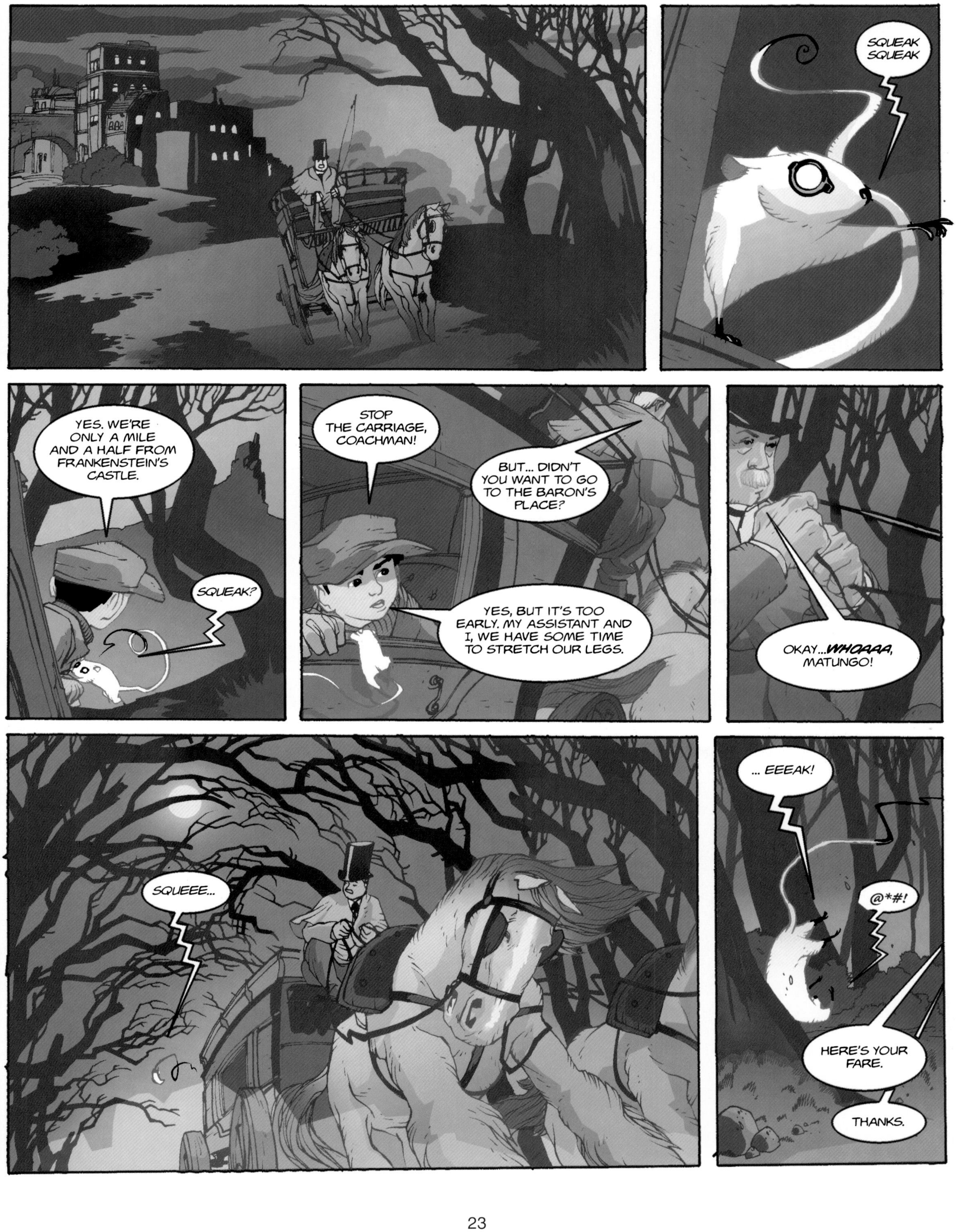
SQUEAK SQUEAK
YES. WE'RE ONLY A MILE AND A HALF FROM FRANKENSTEIN'S CASTLE.
SQUEAK?
STOP THE CARRIAGE, COACHMAN!
BUT... DIDN'T YOU WANT TO GO TO THE BARON'S PLACE?
YES, BUT IT'S TOO EARLY. MY ASSISTANT AND I, WE HAVE SOME TIME TO STRETCH OUR LEGS.
OKAY...WHOAAA, MATUNGO!
SQUEEE...
... EEEAK!
@*#!
HERE'S YOUR FARE.
THANKS.

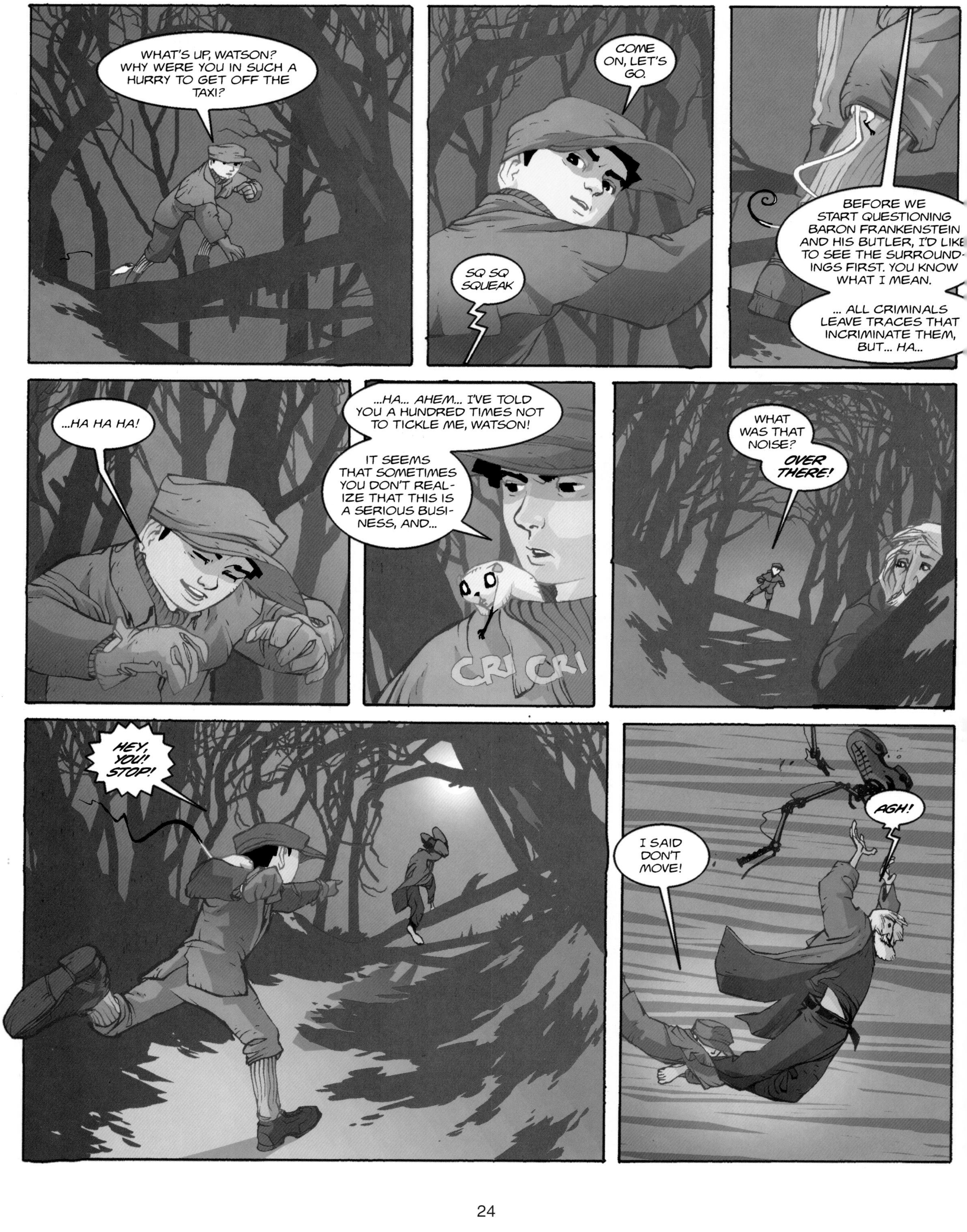
WHAT'S UP, WATSON? WHY WERE YOU IN SUCH A HURRY TO GET OFF THE TAXI?
COME ON, LET'S GO.
SQ SQ SQUEAK
BEFORE WE START QUESTIONING BARON FRANKENSTEIN AND HIS BUTLER, I'D LIKE TO SEE THE SURROUNDINGS FIRST. YOU KNOW WHAT I MEAN.
... ALL CRIMINALS LEAVE TRACES THAT INCRIMINATE THEM, BUT... HA...
...HA HA HA!
...HA... AHEM... I'VE TOLD YOU A HUNDRED TIMES NOT TO TICKLE ME, WATSON!
IT SEEMS THAT SOMETIMES YOU DON'T REALIZE THAT THIS IS A SERIOUS BUSINESS, AND...
CRI CRI
WHAT WAS THAT NOISE?
OVER THERE!
HEY, YOU! STOP!
AGH!
I SAID DON'T MOVE!

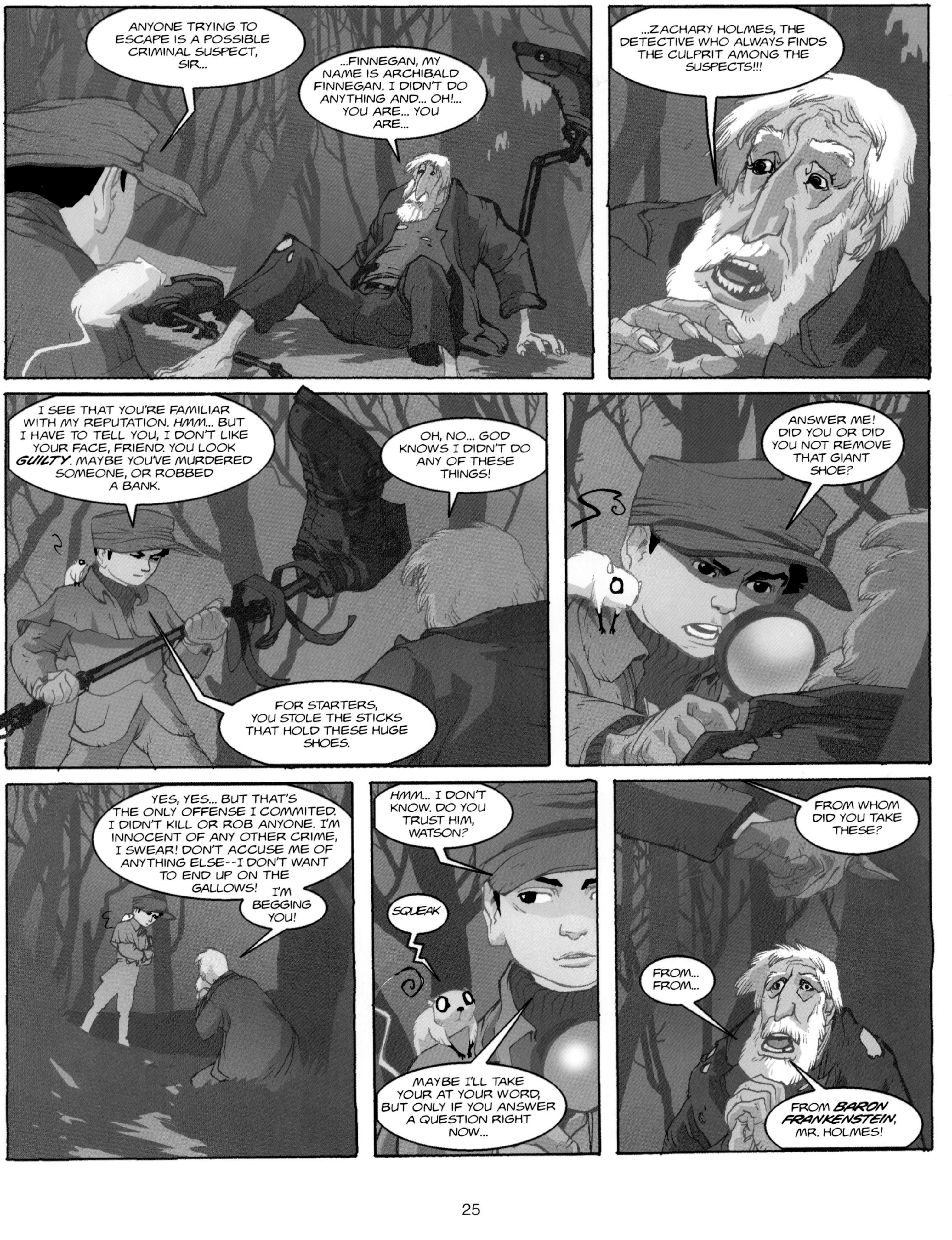
ANYONE TRYING TO ESCAPE IS A POSSIBLE CRIMINAL SUSPECT, SIR...
...FINNEGAN, MY NAME IS ARCHIBALD FINNEGAN. I DIDN'T DO ANYTHING AND... OH!... YOU ARE... YOU ARE...
...ZACHARY HOLMES, THE DETECTIVE WHO ALWAYS FINDS THE CULPRIT AMONG THE SUSPECTS!!!
I SEE THAT YOU'RE FAMILIAR WITH MY REPUTATION. HMM... BUT I HAVE TO TELL YOU, I DON'T LIKE YOUR FACE, FRIEND. YOU LOOK GUILTY. MAYBE YOU'VE MURDERED SOMEONE, OR ROBBED A BANK.
OH, NO... GOD KNOWS I DIDN'T DO ANY OF THESE THINGS!
FOR STARTERS, YOU STOLE THE STICKS THAT HOLD THESE HUGE SHOES.
ANSWER ME! DID YOU OR DID YOU NOT REMOVE THAT GIANT SHOE?
YES, YES... BUT THAT'S THE ONLY OFFENSE I COMMITED. I DIDN'T KILL OR ROB ANYONE. I'M INNOCENT OF ANY OTHER CRIME, I SWEAR! DON'T ACCUSE ME OF ANYTHING ELSE--I DON'T WANT TO END UP ON THE GALLOWS!
I'M BEGGING YOU!
HMM... I DON'T KNOW. DO YOU TRUST HIM, WATSON?
SQUEAK
MAYBE I'LL TAKE YOUR AT YOUR WORD, BUT ONLY IF YOU ANSWER A QUESTION RIGHT NOW...
FROM WHOM DID YOU TAKE THESE?
FROM... FROM...
FROM BARON FRANKENSTEIN, MR. HOLMES!

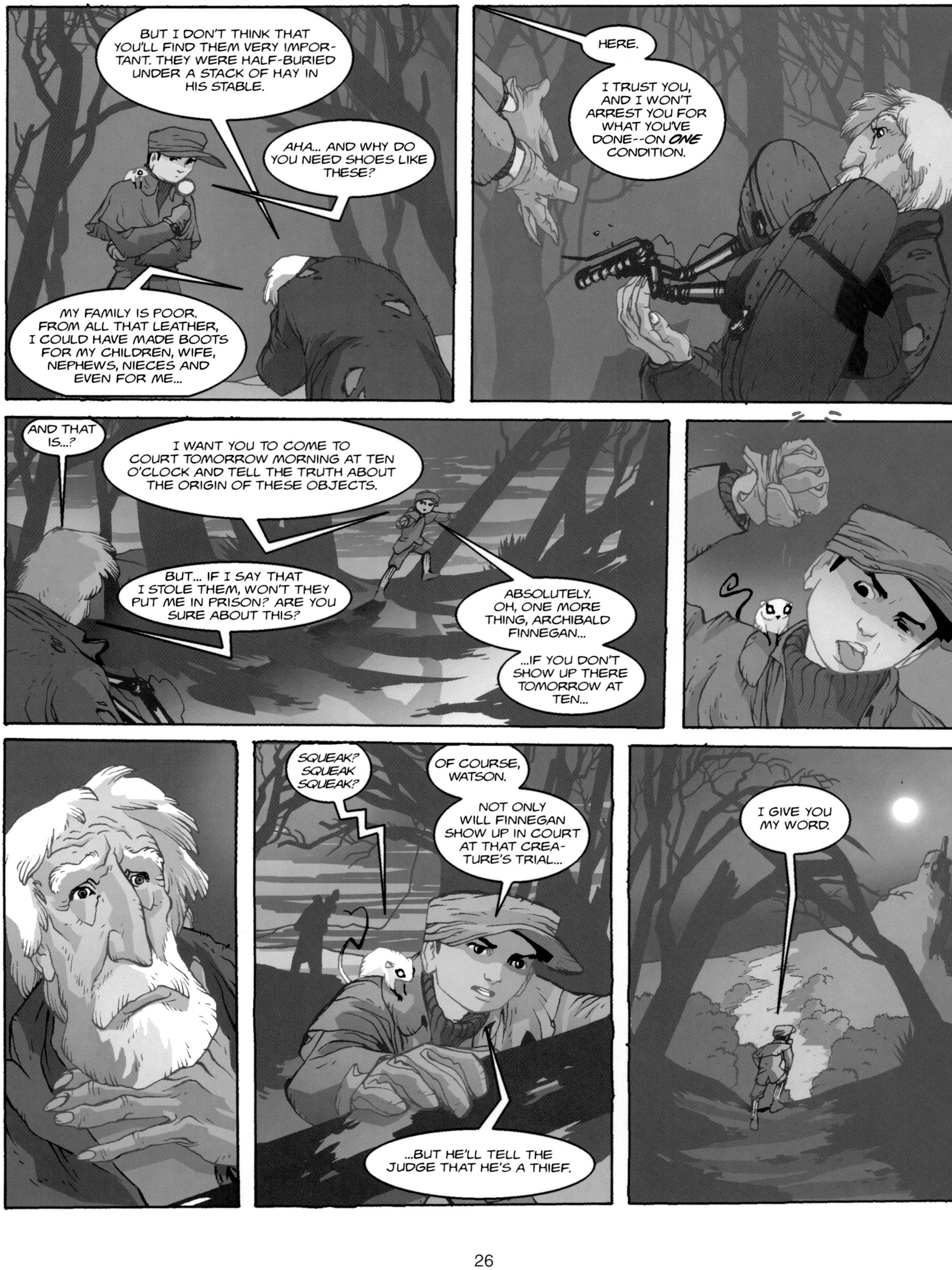
BUT I DON'T THINK THAT YOU'LL FIND THEM VERY IMPORTANT. THEY WERE HALF-BURIED UNDER A STACK OF HAY IN HIS STABLE.
AHA... AND WHY DO YOU NEED SHOES LIKE THESE?
MY FAMILY IS POOR. FROM ALL THAT LEATHER, I COULD HAVE MADE BOOTS FOR MY CHILDREN, WIFE, NEPHEWS, NIECES AND EVEN FOR ME...
HERE.
I TRUST YOU, AND I WON'T ARREST YOU FOR WHAT YOU'VE DONE--ON ONE CONDITION.
AND THAT IS...?
I WANT YOU TO COME TO COURT TOMORROW MORNING AT TEN O'CLOCK AND TELL THE TRUTH ABOUT THE ORIGIN OF THESE OBJECTS.
BUT... IF I SAY THAT I STOLE THEM, WON'T THEY PUT ME IN PRISON? ARE YOU SURE ABOUT THIS?
ABSOLUTELY. OH, ONE MORE THING, ARCHIBALD FINNEGAN...
...IF YOU DON'T SHOW UP THERE TOMORROW AT TEN...
SQUEAK? SQUEAK SQUEAK?
OF COURSE, WATSON.
NOT ONLY WILL FINNEGAN SHOW UP IN COURT AT THAT CREATURE'S TRIAL...
...BUT HE'LL TELL THE JUDGE THAT HE'S A THIEF.
I GIVE YOU MY WORD.

AND NOW LET'S ASK BARON FRANKENSTEIN SOME QUESTIONS, BECAUSE THERE ARE SOME UNCLEAR POINTS THAT--

WATSON...? IF HE DOESN'T START SHOWING MORE INTEREST IN THE JOB, I'LL FIND MYSELF ANOTHER ASSISTANT.

TOC TOC

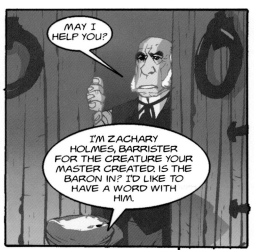

MAY I HELP YOU?

I'M ZACHARY HOLMES, BARRISTER FOR THE CREATURE YOUR MASTER CREATED. IS THE BARON IN? I'D LIKE TO HAVE A WORD WITH HIM.

BSBSBS BSLOESPERABSSBS HOLMESBSBS...

WHAT ARE YOU SAYING, IGOR?

THAT SOME DAMNED *MERCENARY* IS DEFENDING THAT *SCUM* I UNFORTUNATELY CREATED?!

DON'T TAKE IT TO HEART, MY LORD...

STOP IT, FOR HEAVEN'S SAKE!

GET AWAY, IGOR! ANYONE WHO TRIES TO PROVE THE INNOCENCE OF THAT MURDERING BEAST BECOMES MY *MORTAL ENEMY!*

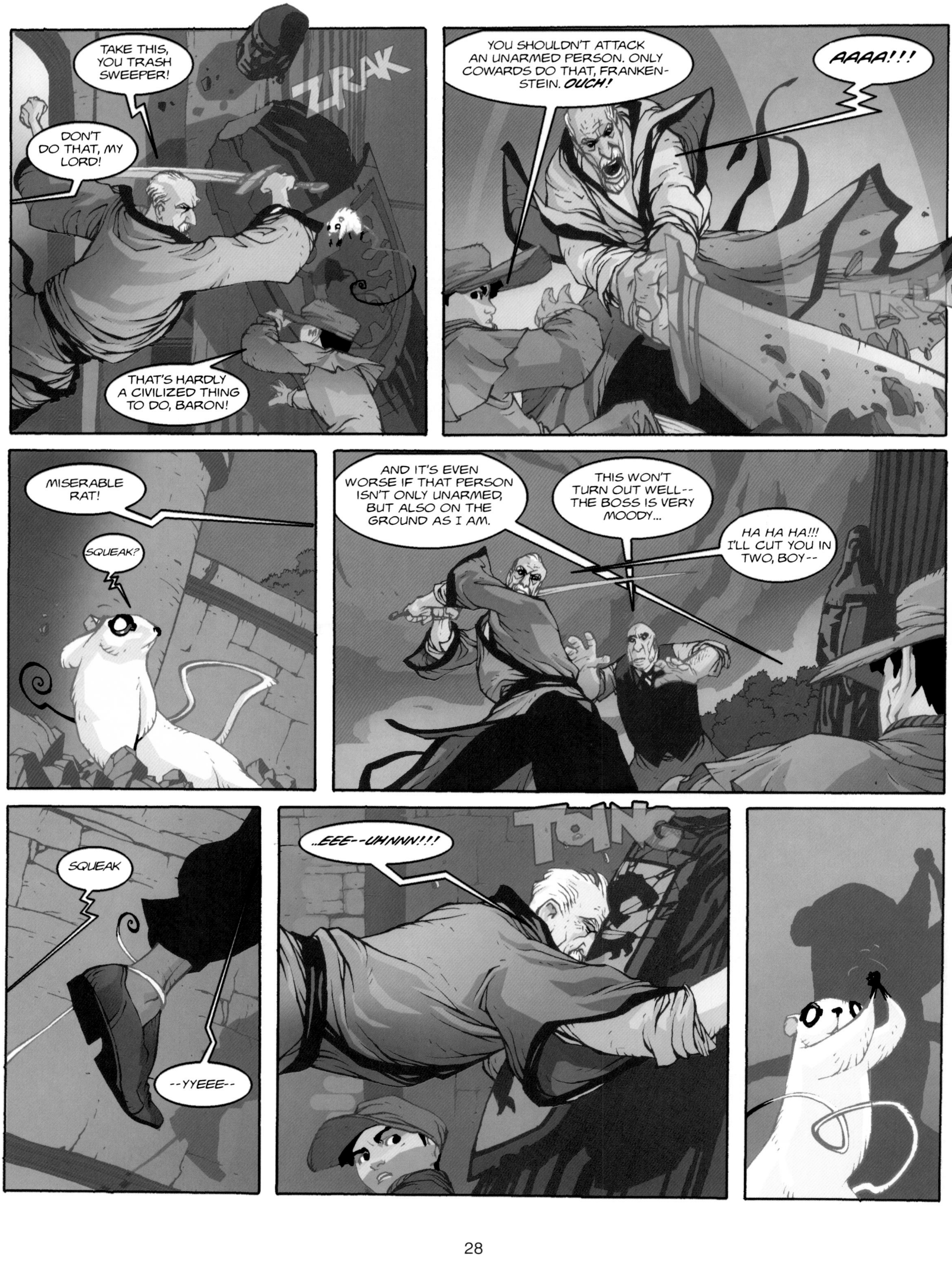
TAKE THIS, YOU TRASH SWEEPER!
ZRAK
DON'T DO THAT, MY LORD!
THAT'S HARDLY A CIVILIZED THING TO DO, BARON!
YOU SHOULDN'T ATTACK AN UNARMED PERSON. ONLY COWARDS DO THAT, FRANKEN-STEIN. OUCH!
AAAA!!!
MISERABLE RAT!
SQUEAK?
AND IT'S EVEN WORSE IF THAT PERSON ISN'T ONLY UNARMED, BUT ALSO ON THE GROUND AS I AM.
THIS WON'T TURN OUT WELL-- THE BOSS IS VERY MOODY...
HA HA HA!!! I'LL CUT YOU IN TWO, BOY--
SQUEAK
--YYEEE--
TOING
..EEE--UHNNN!!!

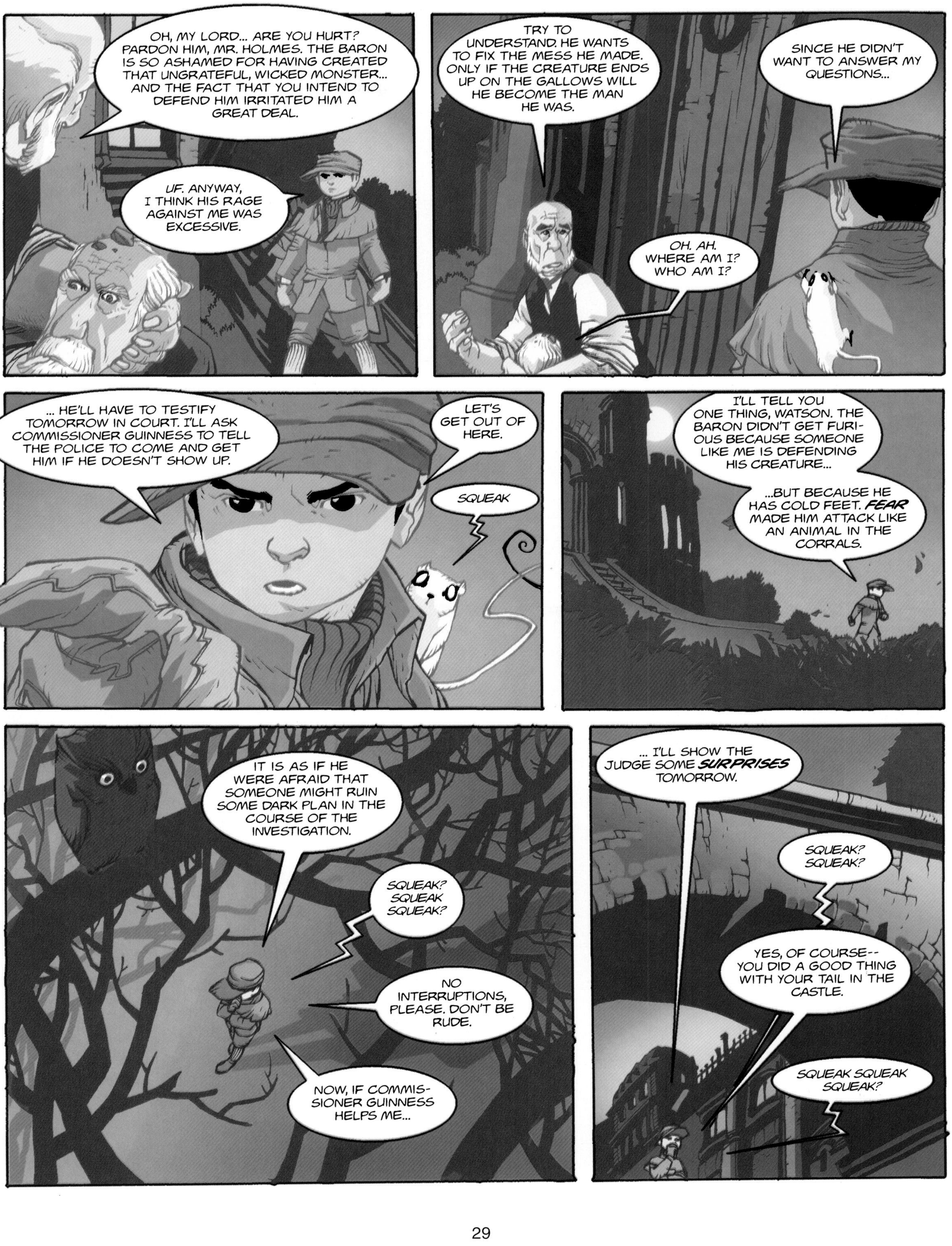
OH, MY LORD... ARE YOU HURT? PARDON HIM, MR. HOLMES. THE BARON IS SO ASHAMED FOR HAVING CREATED THAT UNGRATEFUL, WICKED MONSTER... AND THE FACT THAT YOU INTEND TO DEFEND HIM IRRITATED HIM A GREAT DEAL.
UF. ANYWAY, I THINK HIS RAGE AGAINST ME WAS EXCESSIVE.
TRY TO UNDERSTAND. HE WANTS TO FIX THE MESS HE MADE. ONLY IF THE CREATURE ENDS UP ON THE GALLOWS WILL HE BECOME THE MAN HE WAS.
OH. AH. WHERE AM I? WHO AM I?
SINCE HE DIDN'T WANT TO ANSWER MY QUESTIONS...
... HE'LL HAVE TO TESTIFY TOMORROW IN COURT. I'LL ASK COMMISSIONER GUINNESS TO TELL THE POLICE TO COME AND GET HIM IF HE DOESN'T SHOW UP.
LET'S GET OUT OF HERE.
SQUEAK
I'LL TELL YOU ONE THING, WATSON. THE BARON DIDN'T GET FURI-OUS BECAUSE SOMEONE LIKE ME IS DEFENDING HIS CREATURE...
...BUT BECAUSE HE HAS COLD FEET. FEAR MADE HIM ATTACK LIKE AN ANIMAL IN THE CORRALS.
IT IS AS IF HE WERE AFRAID THAT SOMEONE MIGHT RUIN SOME DARK PLAN IN THE COURSE OF THE INVESTIGATION.
SQUEAK? SQUEAK SQUEAK?
NO INTERRUPTIONS, PLEASE. DON'T BE RUDE.
NOW, IF COMMIS-SIONER GUINNESS HELPS ME...
... I'LL SHOW THE JUDGE SOME SURPRISES TOMORROW.
SQUEAK? SQUEAK?
YES, OF COURSE-- YOU DID A GOOD THING WITH YOUR TAIL IN THE CASTLE.
SQUEAK SQUEAK SQUEAK?

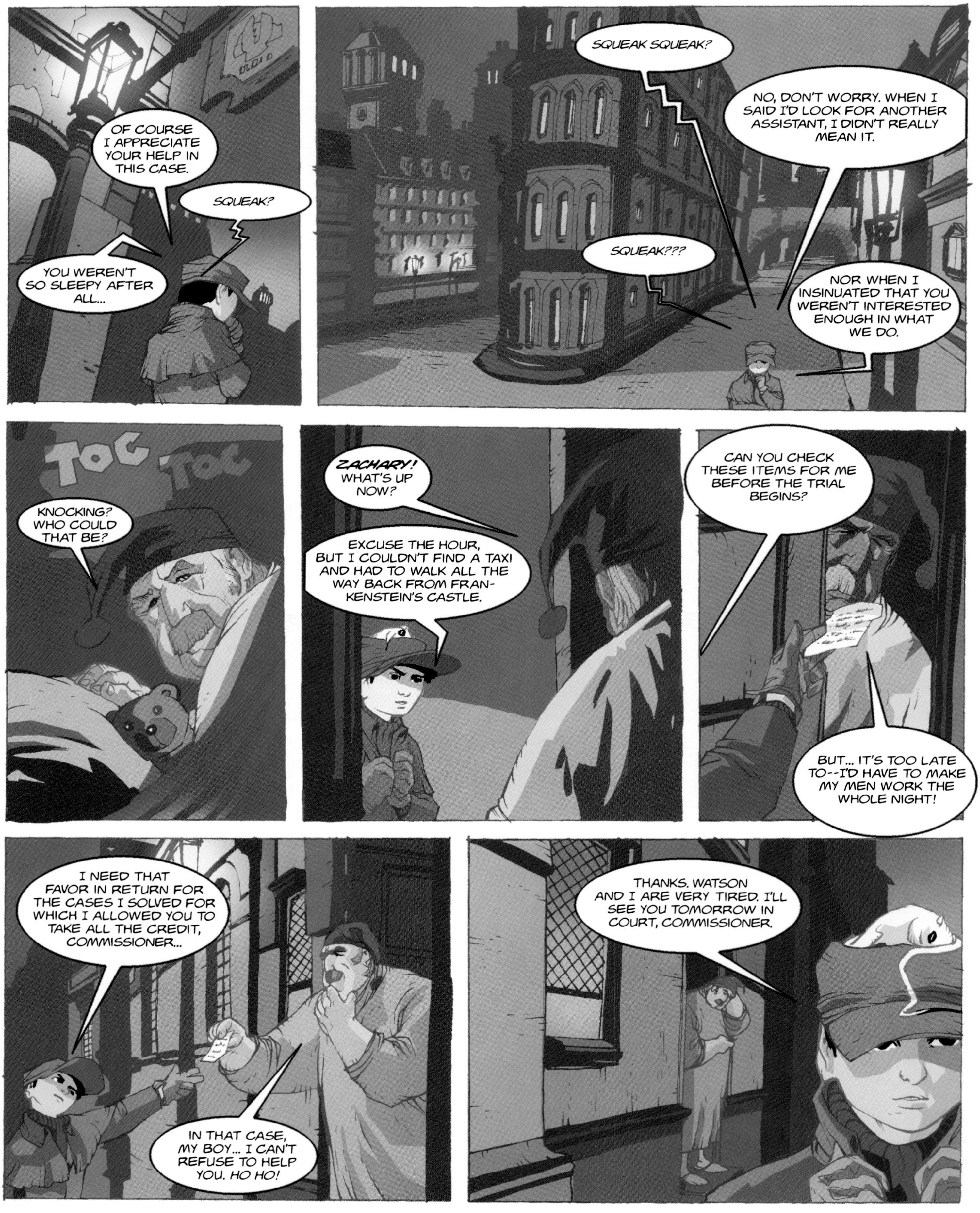
OF COURSE I APPRECIATE YOUR HELP IN THIS CASE.
SQUEAK?
YOU WEREN'T SO SLEEPY AFTER ALL...
SQUEAK SQUEAK?
NO, DON'T WORRY. WHEN I SAID I'D LOOK FOR ANOTHER ASSISTANT, I DIDN'T REALLY MEAN IT.
SQUEAK???
NOR WHEN I INSINUATED THAT YOU WEREN'T INTERESTED ENOUGH IN WHAT WE DO.
TOC TOC
KNOCKING? WHO COULD THAT BE?
ZACHARY! WHAT'S UP NOW?
EXCUSE THE HOUR, BUT I COULDN'T FIND A TAXI AND HAD TO WALK ALL THE WAY BACK FROM FRANKENSTEIN'S CASTLE.
CAN YOU CHECK THESE ITEMS FOR ME BEFORE THE TRIAL BEGINS?
BUT... IT'S TOO LATE TO--I'D HAVE TO MAKE MY MEN WORK THE WHOLE NIGHT!
I NEED THAT FAVOR IN RETURN FOR THE CASES I SOLVED FOR WHICH I ALLOWED YOU TO TAKE ALL THE CREDIT, COMMISSIONER...
IN THAT CASE, MY BOY... I CAN'T REFUSE TO HELP YOU. HO HO!
THANKS. WATSON AND I ARE VERY TIRED. I'LL SEE YOU TOMORROW IN COURT, COMMISSIONER.

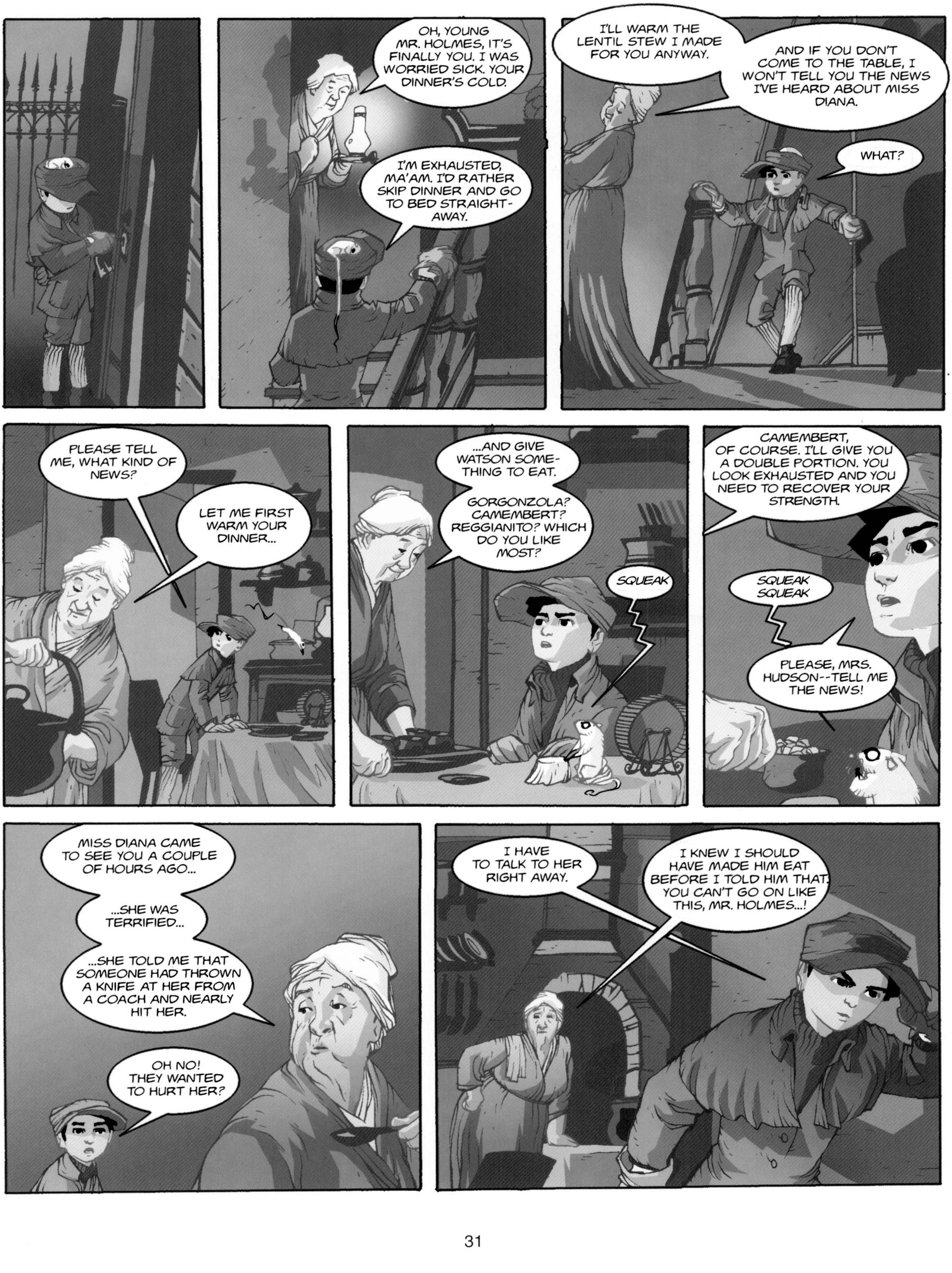
OH, YOUNG MR. HOLMES, IT'S FINALLY YOU. I WAS WORRIED SICK. YOUR DINNER'S COLD.
I'M EXHAUSTED, MA'AM. I'D RATHER SKIP DINNER AND GO TO BED STRAIGHT-AWAY.
I'LL WARM THE LENTIL STEW I MADE FOR YOU ANYWAY.
AND IF YOU DON'T COME TO THE TABLE, I WON'T TELL YOU THE NEWS I'VE HEARD ABOUT MISS DIANA.
WHAT?
PLEASE TELL ME, WHAT KIND OF NEWS?
LET ME FIRST WARM YOUR DINNER...
...AND GIVE WATSON SOME-THING TO EAT.
GORGONZOLA? CAMEMBERT? REGGIANITO? WHICH DO YOU LIKE MOST?
SQUEAK
CAMEMBERT, OF COURSE. I'LL GIVE YOU A DOUBLE PORTION. YOU LOOK EXHAUSTED AND YOU NEED TO RECOVER YOUR STRENGTH.
SQUEAK SQUEAK
PLEASE, MRS. HUDSON--TELL ME THE NEWS!
MISS DIANA CAME TO SEE YOU A COUPLE OF HOURS AGO...
...SHE WAS TERRIFIED...
...SHE TOLD ME THAT SOMEONE HAD THROWN A KNIFE AT HER FROM A COACH AND NEARLY HIT HER.
OH NO! THEY WANTED TO HURT HER?
I HAVE TO TALK TO HER RIGHT AWAY.
I KNEW I SHOULD HAVE MADE HIM EAT BEFORE I TOLD HIM THAT. YOU CAN'T GO ON LIKE THIS, MR. HOLMES...!

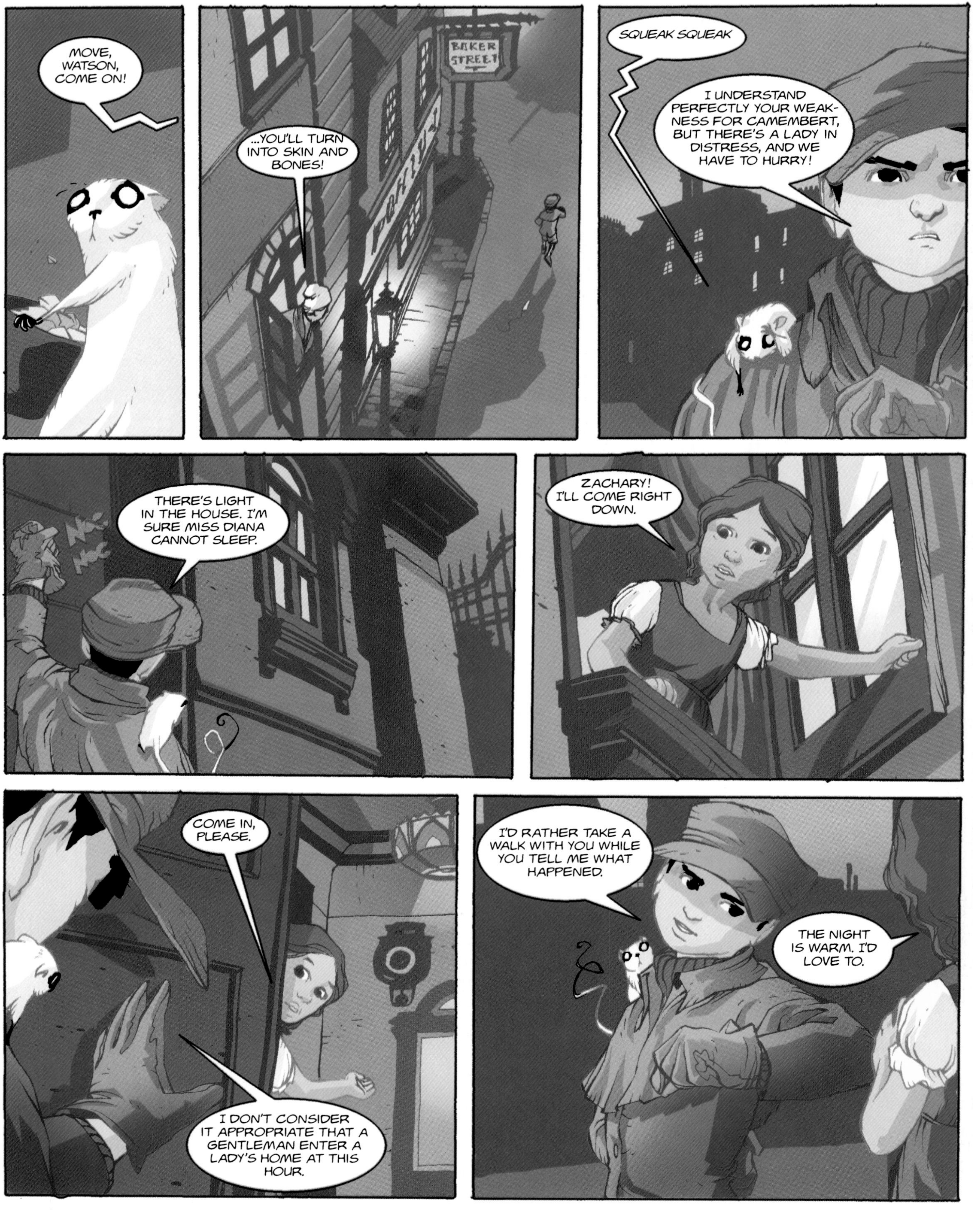
MOVE, WATSON, COME ON!
BAKER STREET
...YOU'LL TURN INTO SKIN AND BONES!
SQUEAK SQUEAK
I UNDERSTAND PERFECTLY YOUR WEAKNESS FOR CAMEMBERT, BUT THERE'S A LADY IN DISTRESS, AND WE HAVE TO HURRY!
THERE'S LIGHT IN THE HOUSE. I'M SURE MISS DIANA CANNOT SLEEP.
ZACHARY! I'LL COME RIGHT DOWN.
COME IN, PLEASE.
I DON'T CONSIDER IT APPROPRIATE THAT A GENTLEMAN ENTER A LADY'S HOME AT THIS HOUR.
I'D RATHER TAKE A WALK WITH YOU WHILE YOU TELL ME WHAT HAPPENED.
THE NIGHT IS WARM. I'D LOVE TO.

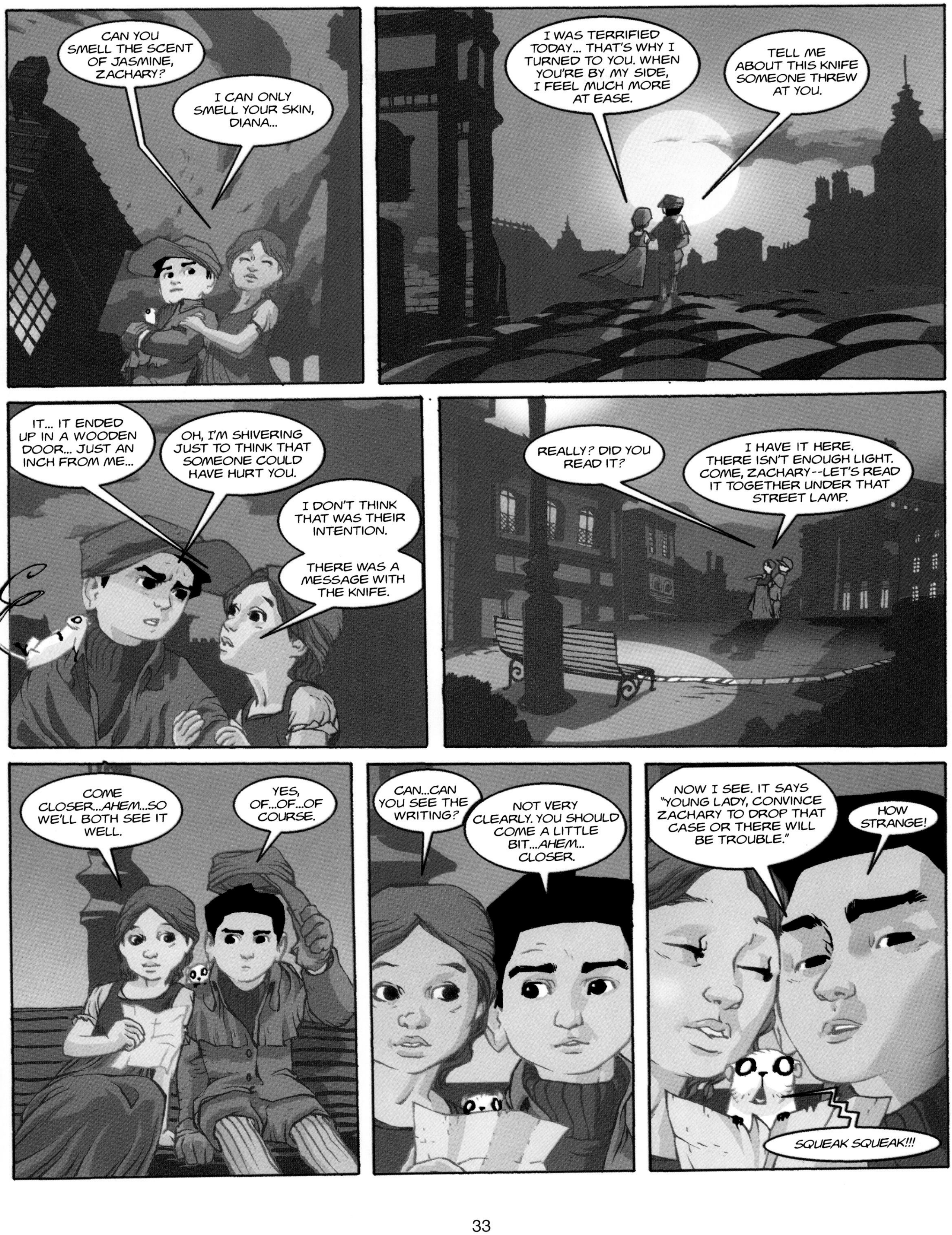
CAN YOU SMELL THE SCENT OF JASMINE, ZACHARY?
I CAN ONLY SMELL YOUR SKIN, DIANA...
I WAS TERRIFIED TODAY... THAT'S WHY I TURNED TO YOU. WHEN YOU'RE BY MY SIDE, I FEEL MUCH MORE AT EASE.
TELL ME ABOUT THIS KNIFE SOMEONE THREW AT YOU.
IT... IT ENDED UP IN A WOODEN DOOR... JUST AN INCH FROM ME...
OH, I'M SHIVERING JUST TO THINK THAT SOMEONE COULD HAVE HURT YOU.
I DON'T THINK THAT WAS THEIR INTENTION.
THERE WAS A MESSAGE WITH THE KNIFE.
REALLY? DID YOU READ IT?
I HAVE IT HERE. THERE ISN'T ENOUGH LIGHT. COME, ZACHARY--LET'S READ IT TOGETHER UNDER THAT STREET LAMP.
COME CLOSER...AHEM...SO WE'LL BOTH SEE IT WELL.
YES, OF...OF...OF COURSE.
CAN...CAN YOU SEE THE WRITING?
NOT VERY CLEARLY. YOU SHOULD COME A LITTLE BIT...AHEM... CLOSER.
NOW I SEE. IT SAYS "YOUNG LADY, CONVINCE ZACHARY TO DROP THAT CASE OR THERE WILL BE TROUBLE."
HOW STRANGE!
SQUEAK SQUEAK!!!

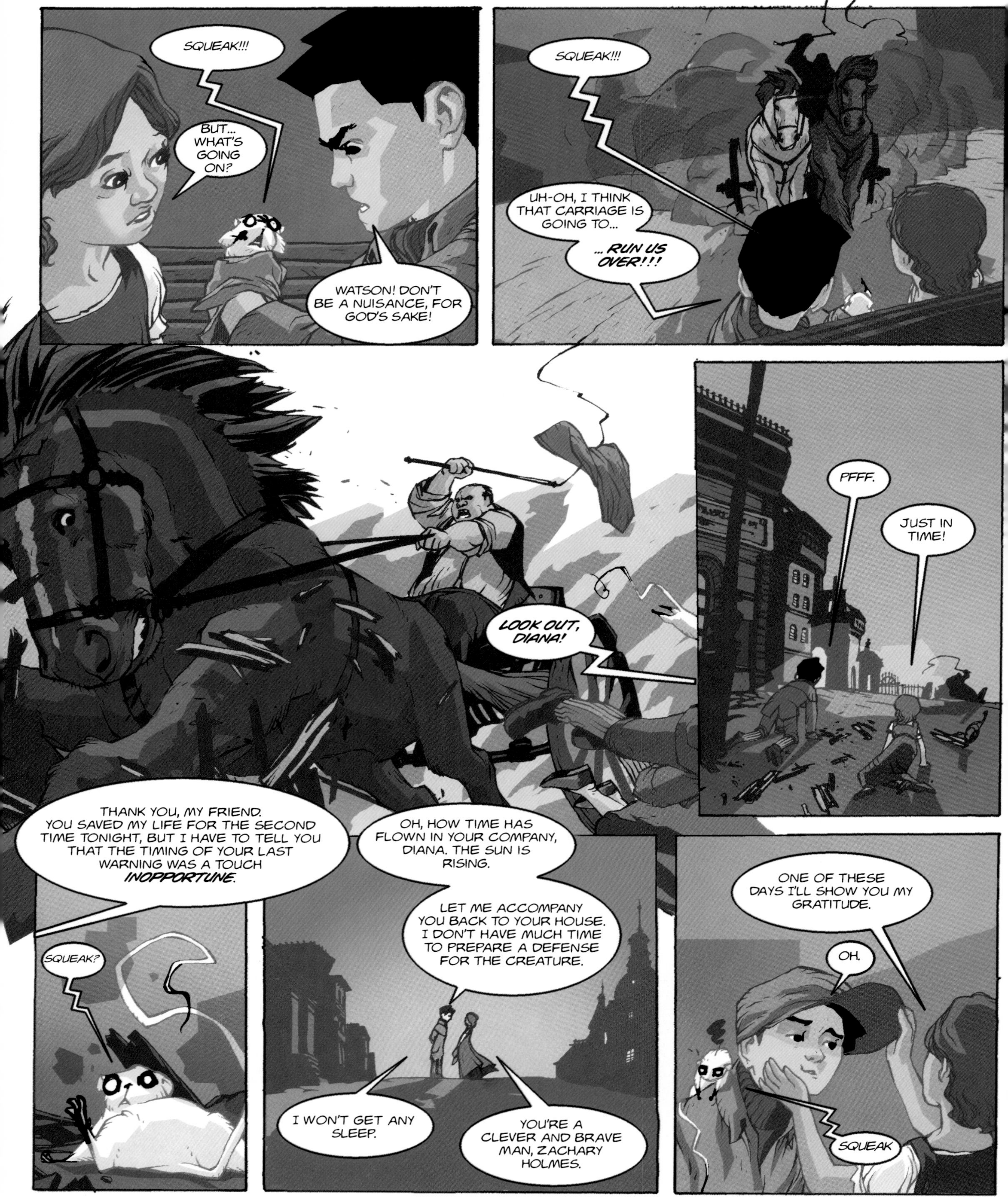
SQUEAK!!!
BUT... WHAT'S GOING ON?
WATSON! DON'T BE A NUISANCE, FOR GOD'S SAKE!
SQUEAK!!!
UH-OH, I THINK THAT CARRIAGE IS GOING TO...
... RUN US OVER!!!
LOOK OUT, DIANA!
PFFF.
JUST IN TIME!
THANK YOU, MY FRIEND. YOU SAVED MY LIFE FOR THE SECOND TIME TONIGHT, BUT I HAVE TO TELL YOU THAT THE TIMING OF YOUR LAST WARNING WAS A TOUCH INOPPORTUNE.
SQUEAK?
OH, HOW TIME HAS FLOWN IN YOUR COMPANY, DIANA. THE SUN IS RISING.
LET ME ACCOMPANY YOU BACK TO YOUR HOUSE. I DON'T HAVE MUCH TIME TO PREPARE A DEFENSE FOR THE CREATURE.
I WON'T GET ANY SLEEP.
YOU'RE A CLEVER AND BRAVE MAN, ZACHARY HOLMES.
ONE OF THESE DAYS I'LL SHOW YOU MY GRATITUDE.
OH.
SQUEAK

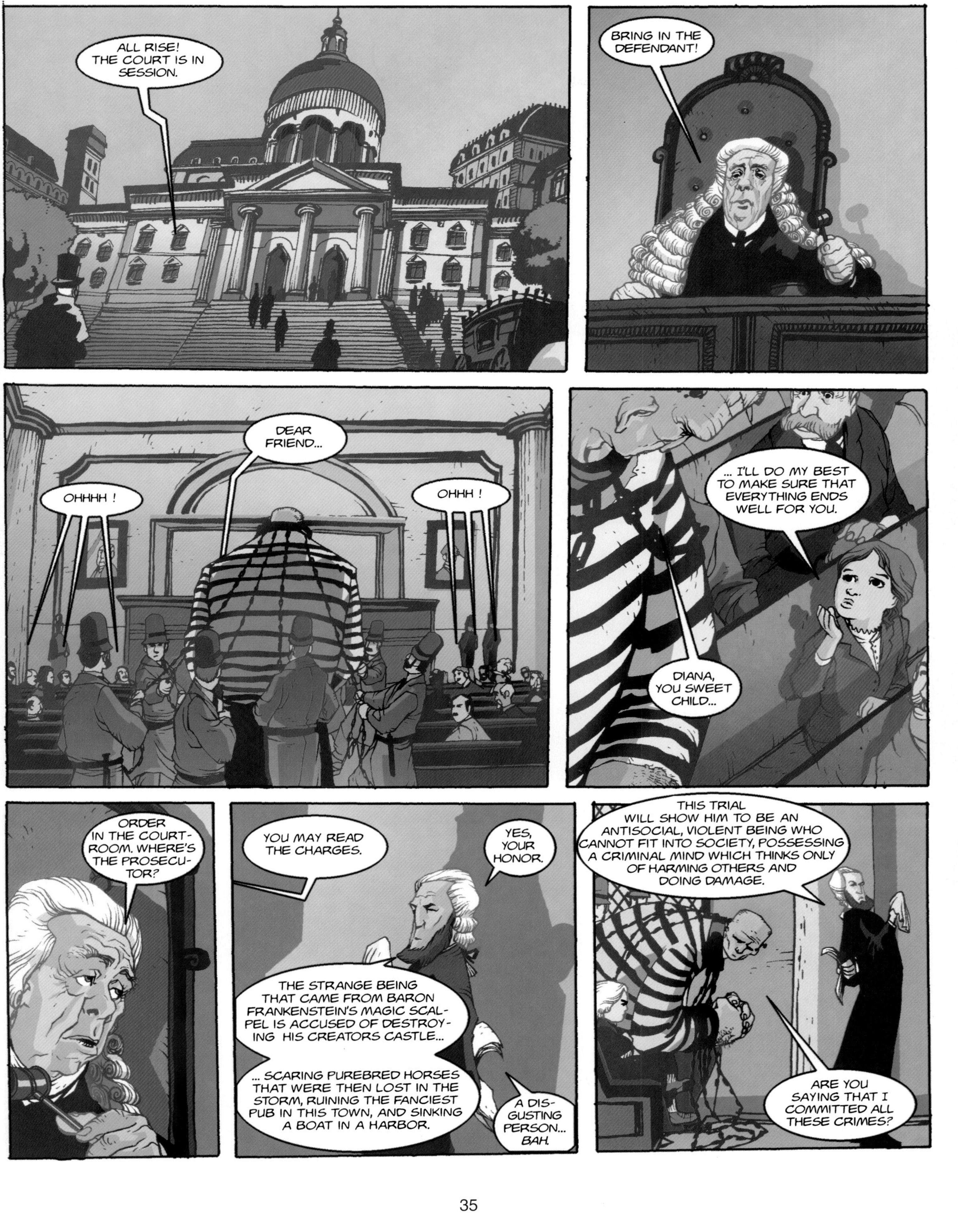
ALL RISE! THE COURT IS IN SESSION.
BRING IN THE DEFENDANT!
DEAR FRIEND...
OHHHH !
OHHH !
... I'LL DO MY BEST TO MAKE SURE THAT EVERYTHING ENDS WELL FOR YOU.
DIANA, YOU SWEET CHILD...
ORDER IN THE COURT-ROOM. WHERE'S THE PROSECU-TOR?
YOU MAY READ THE CHARGES.
YES, YOUR HONOR.
THE STRANGE BEING THAT CAME FROM BARON FRANKENSTEIN'S MAGIC SCAL-PEL IS ACCUSED OF DESTROY-ING HIS CREATORS CASTLE...
... SCARING PUREBRED HORSES THAT WERE THEN LOST IN THE STORM, RUINING THE FANCIEST PUB IN THIS TOWN, AND SINKING A BOAT IN A HARBOR.
A DIS-GUSTING PERSON... BAH.
THIS TRIAL WILL SHOW HIM TO BE AN ANTISOCIAL, VIOLENT BEING WHO CANNOT FIT INTO SOCIETY, POSSESSING A CRIMINAL MIND WHICH THINKS ONLY OF HARMING OTHERS AND DOING DAMAGE.
ARE YOU SAYING THAT I COMMITTED ALL THESE CRIMES?

OF COURSE, WHO ELSE?

I'LL TELL YOU JUST ONE THING, SIR.

I'M NOT GUILTY OF ANY OF THESE ATROCITIES!!

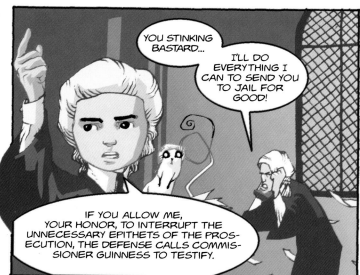

YOU STINKING BASTARD...

I'LL DO EVERYTHING I CAN TO SEND YOU TO JAIL FOR GOOD!

IF YOU ALLOW ME, YOUR HONOR, TO INTERRUPT THE UNNECESSARY EPITHETS OF THE PROSECUTION, THE DEFENSE CALLS COMMISSIONER GUINNESS TO TESTIFY.

WE'RE LISTENING CAREFULLY, COMMISSIONER.

AHEM... MR. HOLMES ASKED ME TO CHECK ON A COUPLE OF THINGS OF WHICH, TO BE HONEST, I HAVE NO IDEA HOW THEY RELATE TO THIS CASE.

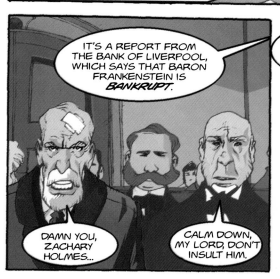

IT'S A REPORT FROM THE BANK OF LIVERPOOL, WHICH SAYS THAT BARON FRANKENSTEIN IS *BANKRUPT*.

DAMN YOU, ZACHARY HOLMES...

CALM DOWN, MY LORD, DON'T INSULT HIM.

HERE'S ANOTHER. THE INSURANCE COMPANY ESTIMATED THE DAMAGE TO THE BARON'S CASTLE TO BE 70,000 POUNDS.

THANK YOU, COMMISSIONER.

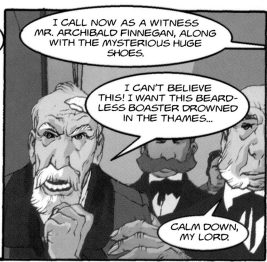

I CALL NOW AS A WITNESS MR. ARCHIBALD FINNEGAN, ALONG WITH THE MYSTERIOUS HUGE SHOES.

I CAN'T BELIEVE THIS! I WANT THIS BEARDLESS BOASTER DROWNED IN THE THAMES...

CALM DOWN, MY LORD.

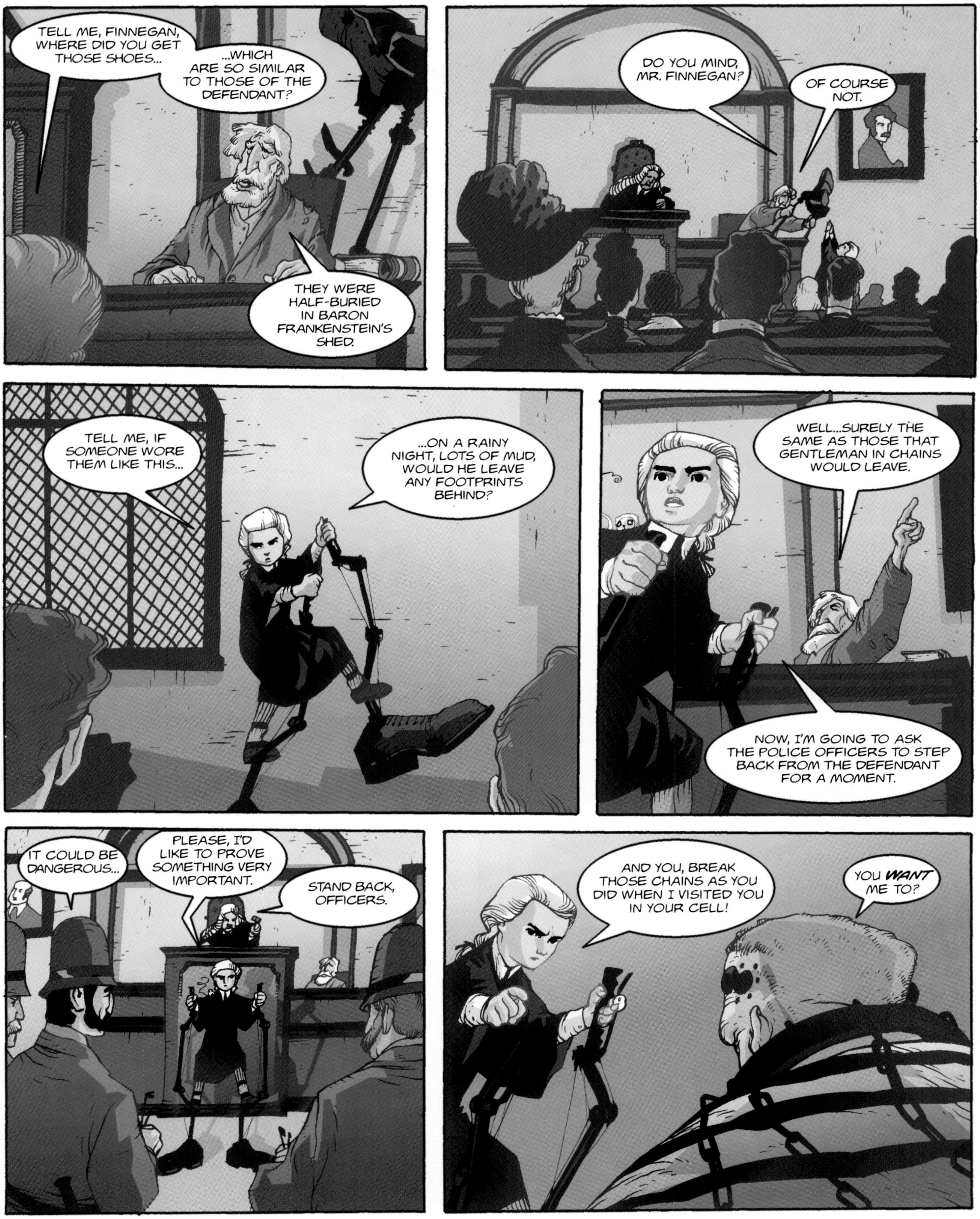
TELL ME, FINNEGAN, WHERE DID YOU GET THOSE SHOES...
...WHICH ARE SO SIMILAR TO THOSE OF THE DEFENDANT?
THEY WERE HALF-BURIED IN BARON FRANKENSTEIN'S SHED.
DO YOU MIND, MR. FINNEGAN?
OF COURSE NOT.
TELL ME, IF SOMEONE WORE THEM LIKE THIS...
...ON A RAINY NIGHT, LOTS OF MUD, WOULD HE LEAVE ANY FOOTPRINTS BEHIND?
WELL...SURELY THE SAME AS THOSE THAT GENTLEMAN IN CHAINS WOULD LEAVE.
NOW, I'M GOING TO ASK THE POLICE OFFICERS TO STEP BACK FROM THE DEFENDANT FOR A MOMENT.
IT COULD BE DANGEROUS...
PLEASE, I'D LIKE TO PROVE SOMETHING VERY IMPORTANT.
STAND BACK, OFFICERS.
AND YOU, BREAK THOSE CHAINS AS YOU DID WHEN I VISITED YOU IN YOUR CELL!
YOU **WANT** ME TO?

VERY WELL.

STAY WHERE YOU ARE, OFFICERS.

AND YOU, SIT DOWN, PLEASE.

YES, SIR. I'M SORRY FOR THIS MESS AND FOR SCARING EVERYONE.

YOU SEE THAT, DON'T YOU? HE COULD HAVE ESCAPED BECAUSE HE'S BEEN *UNCHAINED* FOR SOME TIME NOW.

I DON'T KNOW ANY ANTISOCIAL BEAST WHO BEHAVES SO WELL.

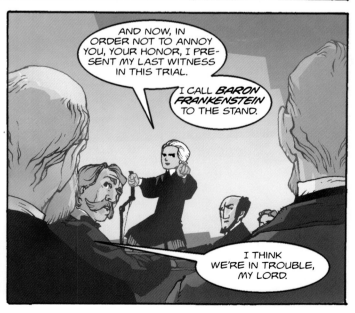

AND NOW, IN ORDER NOT TO ANNOY YOU, YOUR HONOR, I PRESENT MY LAST WITNESS IN THIS TRIAL.

I CALL *BARON FRANKENSTEIN* TO THE STAND.

I THINK WE'RE IN TROUBLE, MY LORD.

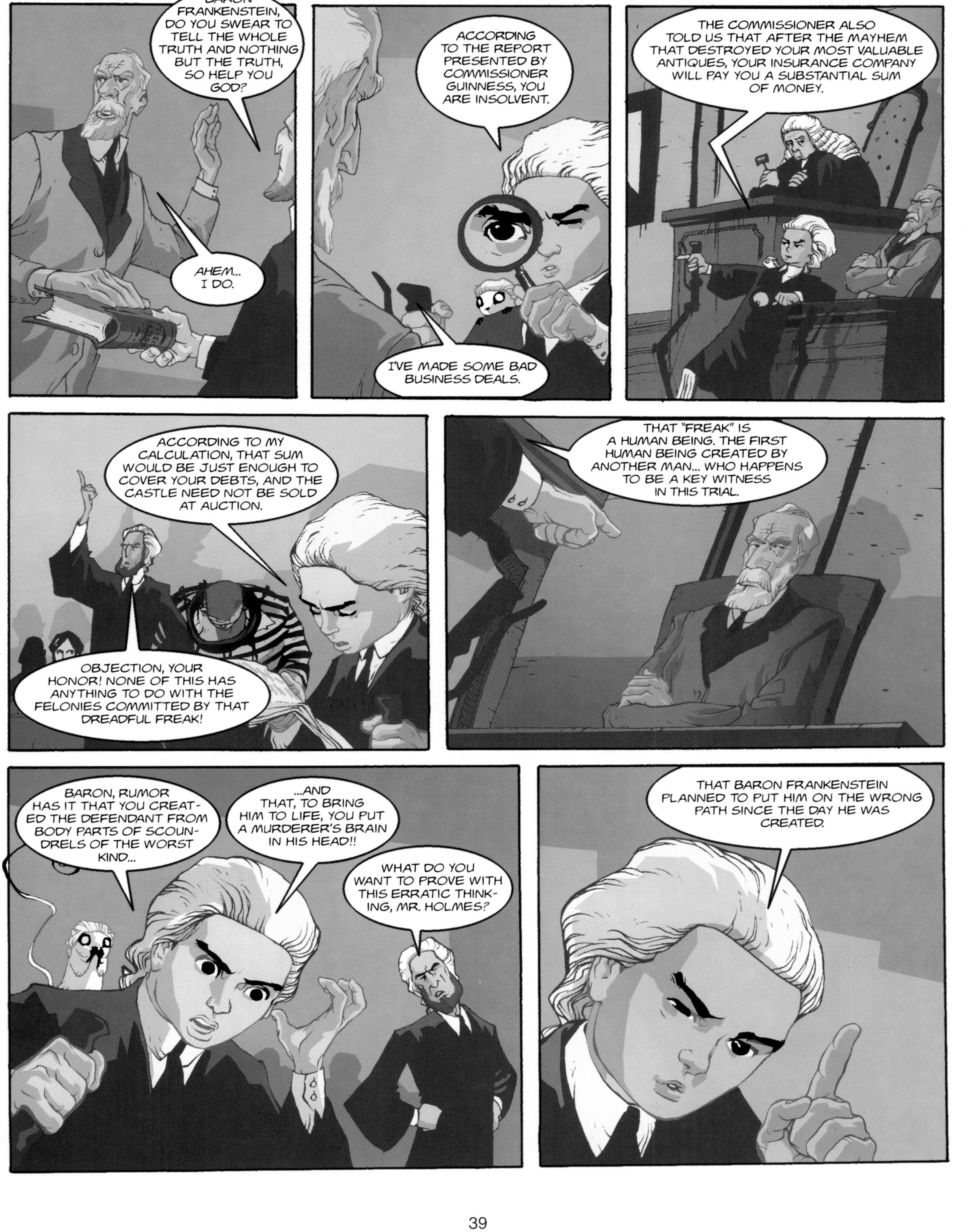
BARON FRANKENSTEIN, DO YOU SWEAR TO TELL THE WHOLE TRUTH AND NOTHING BUT THE TRUTH, SO HELP YOU GOD?
AHEM... I DO.
ACCORDING TO THE REPORT PRESENTED BY COMMISSIONER GUINNESS, YOU ARE INSOLVENT.
I'VE MADE SOME BAD BUSINESS DEALS.
THE COMMISSIONER ALSO TOLD US THAT AFTER THE MAYHEM THAT DESTROYED YOUR MOST VALUABLE ANTIQUES, YOUR INSURANCE COMPANY WILL PAY YOU A SUBSTANTIAL SUM OF MONEY.
ACCORDING TO MY CALCULATION, THAT SUM WOULD BE JUST ENOUGH TO COVER YOUR DEBTS, AND THE CASTLE NEED NOT BE SOLD AT AUCTION.
OBJECTION, YOUR HONOR! NONE OF THIS HAS ANYTHING TO DO WITH THE FELONIES COMMITTED BY THAT DREADFUL FREAK!
THAT "FREAK" IS A HUMAN BEING. THE FIRST HUMAN BEING CREATED BY ANOTHER MAN... WHO HAPPENS TO BE A KEY WITNESS IN THIS TRIAL.
BARON, RUMOR HAS IT THAT YOU CREAT-ED THE DEFENDANT FROM BODY PARTS OF SCOUN-DRELS OF THE WORST KIND...
...AND THAT, TO BRING HIM TO LIFE, YOU PUT A MURDERER'S BRAIN IN HIS HEAD!!
WHAT DO YOU WANT TO PROVE WITH THIS ERRATIC THINK-ING, MR. HOLMES?
THAT BARON FRANKENSTEIN PLANNED TO PUT HIM ON THE WRONG PATH SINCE THE DAY HE WAS CREATED.

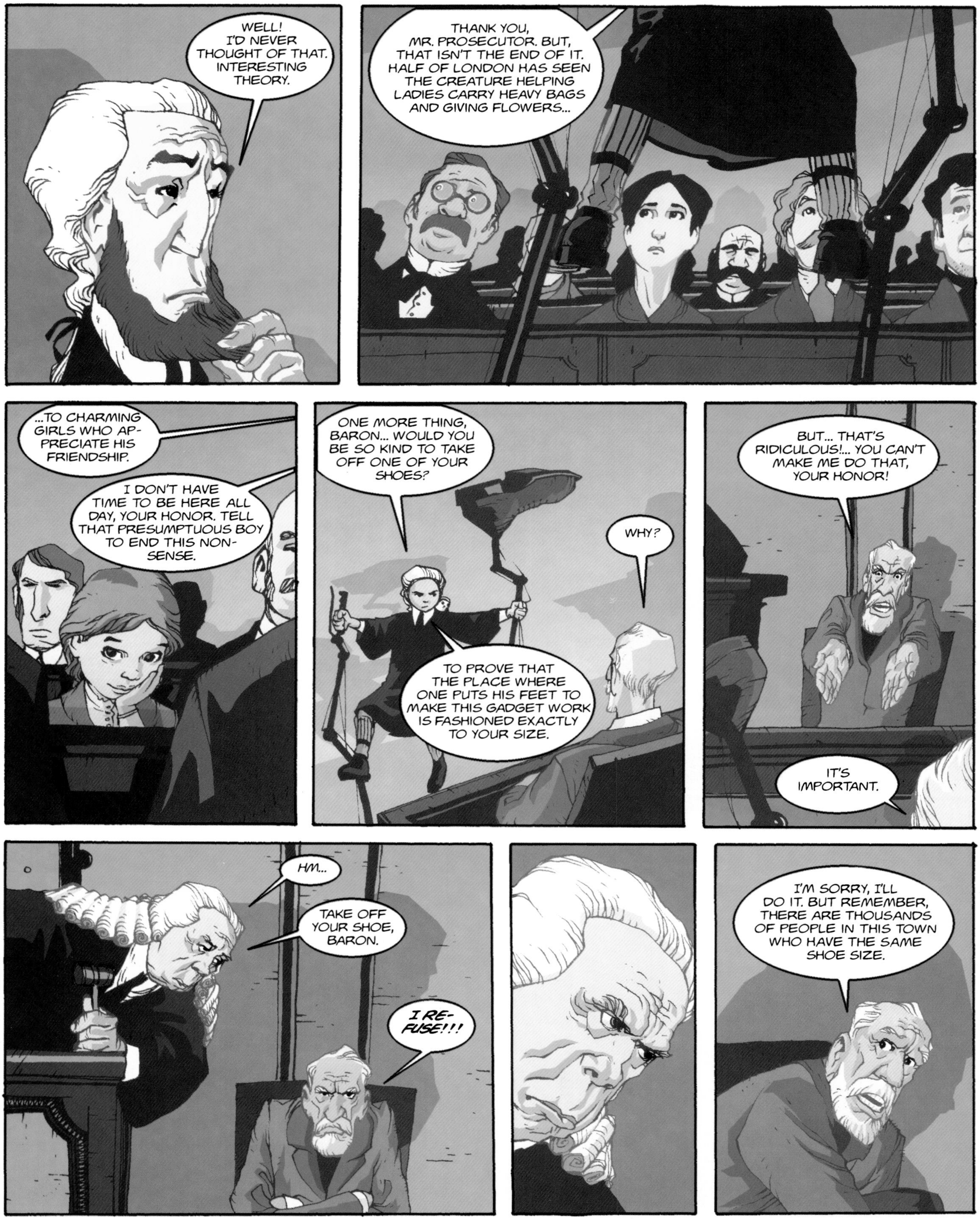
WELL! I'D NEVER THOUGHT OF THAT. INTERESTING THEORY.
THANK YOU, MR. PROSECUTOR. BUT, THAT ISN'T THE END OF IT. HALF OF LONDON HAS SEEN THE CREATURE HELPING LADIES CARRY HEAVY BAGS AND GIVING FLOWERS...
...TO CHARMING GIRLS WHO AP-PRECIATE HIS FRIENDSHIP.
I DON'T HAVE TIME TO BE HERE ALL DAY, YOUR HONOR. TELL THAT PRESUMPTUOUS BOY TO END THIS NON-SENSE.
ONE MORE THING, BARON... WOULD YOU BE SO KIND TO TAKE OFF ONE OF YOUR SHOES?
WHY?
TO PROVE THAT THE PLACE WHERE ONE PUTS HIS FEET TO MAKE THIS GADGET WORK IS FASHIONED EXACTLY TO YOUR SIZE.
BUT... THAT'S RIDICULOUS!... YOU CAN'T MAKE ME DO THAT, YOUR HONOR!
IT'S IMPORTANT.
HM...
TAKE OFF YOUR SHOE, BARON.
I RE-FUSE!!!
I'M SORRY, I'LL DO IT. BUT REMEMBER, THERE ARE THOUSANDS OF PEOPLE IN THIS TOWN WHO HAVE THE SAME SHOE SIZE.

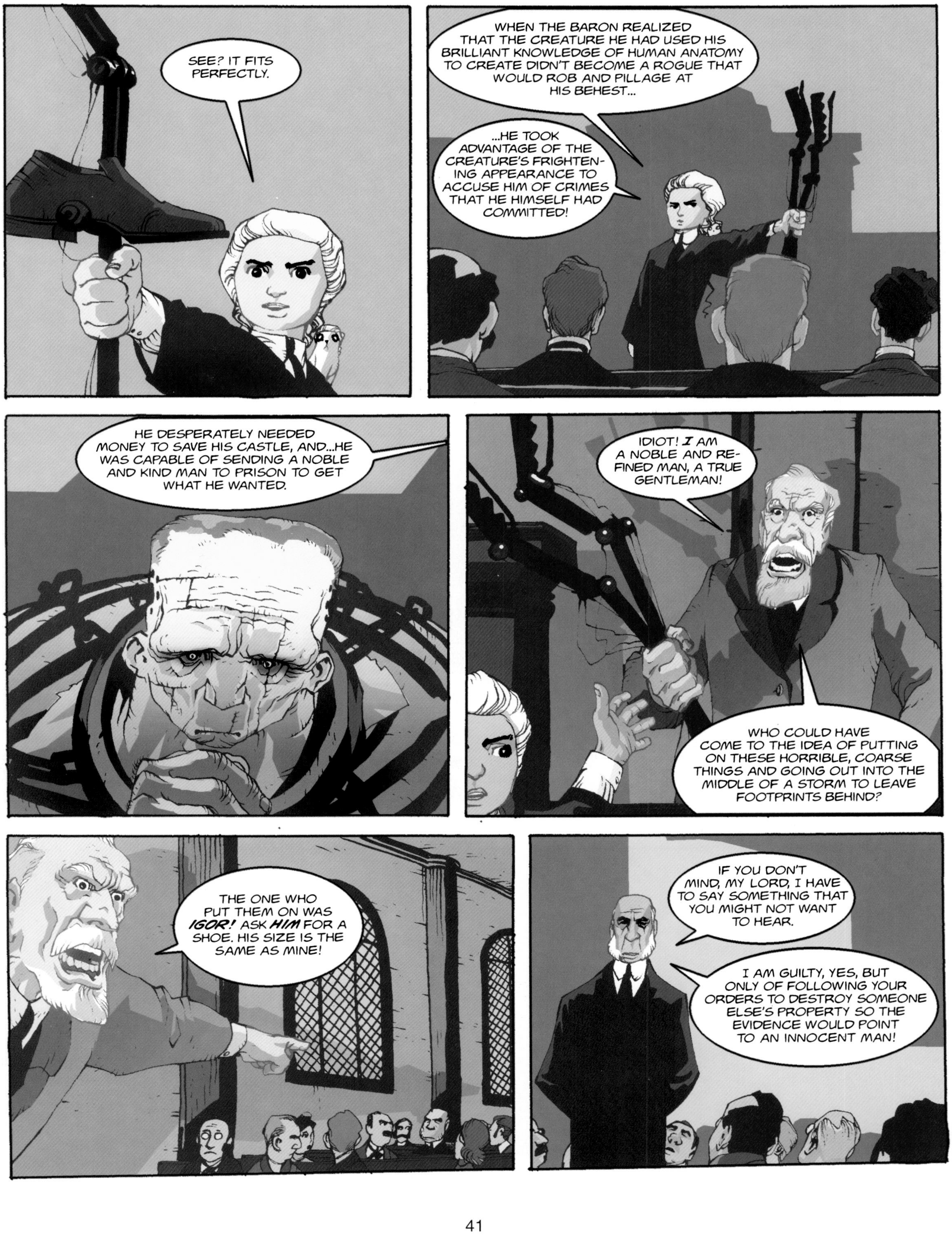
SEE? IT FITS PERFECTLY.
WHEN THE BARON REALIZED THAT THE CREATURE HE HAD USED HIS BRILLIANT KNOWLEDGE OF HUMAN ANATOMY TO CREATE DIDN'T BECOME A ROGUE THAT WOULD ROB AND PILLAGE AT HIS BEHEST...
...HE TOOK ADVANTAGE OF THE CREATURE'S FRIGHTENING APPEARANCE TO ACCUSE HIM OF CRIMES THAT HE HIMSELF HAD COMMITTED!
HE DESPERATELY NEEDED MONEY TO SAVE HIS CASTLE, AND...HE WAS CAPABLE OF SENDING A NOBLE AND KIND MAN TO PRISON TO GET WHAT HE WANTED.
IDIOT! I AM A NOBLE AND REFINED MAN, A TRUE GENTLEMAN!
WHO COULD HAVE COME TO THE IDEA OF PUTTING ON THESE HORRIBLE, COARSE THINGS AND GOING OUT INTO THE MIDDLE OF A STORM TO LEAVE FOOTPRINTS BEHIND?
THE ONE WHO PUT THEM ON WAS IGOR! ASK HIM FOR A SHOE. HIS SIZE IS THE SAME AS MINE!
IF YOU DON'T MIND, MY LORD, I HAVE TO SAY SOMETHING THAT YOU MIGHT NOT WANT TO HEAR.
I AM GUILTY, YES, BUT ONLY OF FOLLOWING YOUR ORDERS TO DESTROY SOMEONE ELSE'S PROPERTY SO THE EVIDENCE WOULD POINT TO AN INNOCENT MAN!

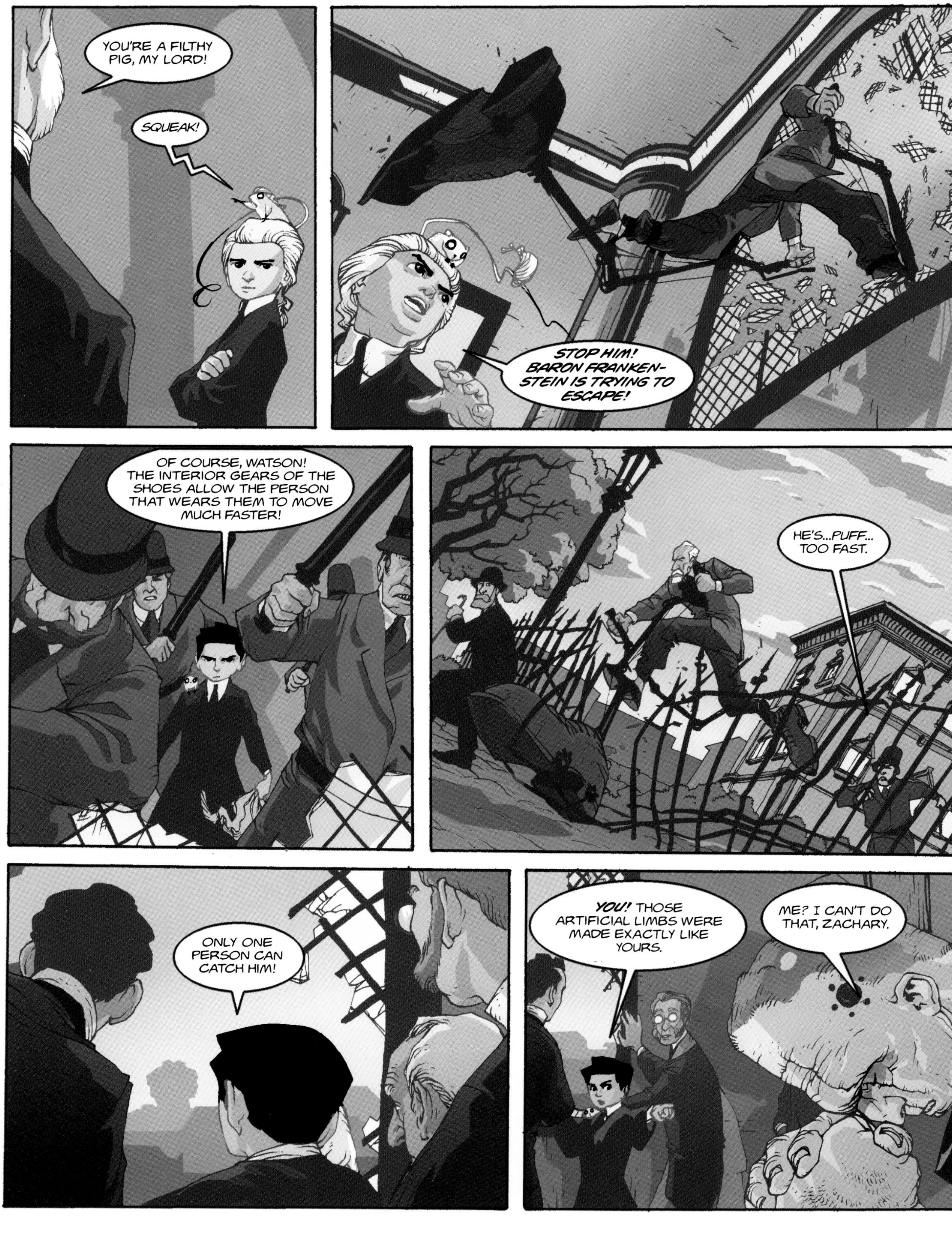
YOU'RE A FILTHY PIG, MY LORD!
SQUEAK!
STOP HIM! BARON FRANKEN-STEIN IS TRYING TO ESCAPE!
OF COURSE, WATSON! THE INTERIOR GEARS OF THE SHOES ALLOW THE PERSON THAT WEARS THEM TO MOVE MUCH FASTER!
HE'S...PUFF... TOO FAST.
ONLY ONE PERSON CAN CATCH HIM!
YOU! THOSE ARTIFICIAL LIMBS WERE MADE EXACTLY LIKE YOURS.
ME? I CAN'T DO THAT, ZACHARY.

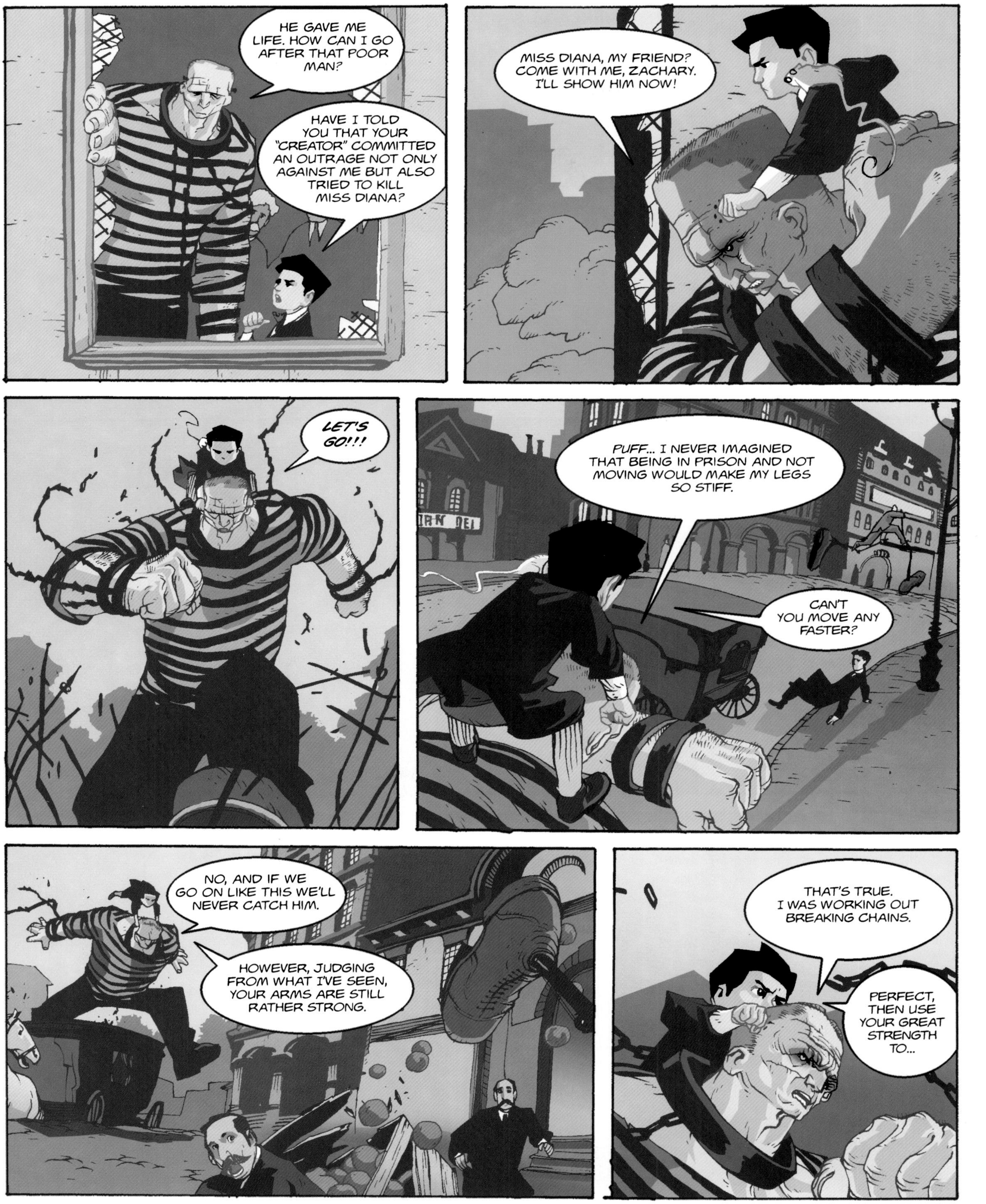
HE GAVE ME LIFE. HOW CAN I GO AFTER THAT POOR MAN?
HAVE I TOLD YOU THAT YOUR "CREATOR" COMMITTED AN OUTRAGE NOT ONLY AGAINST ME BUT ALSO TRIED TO KILL MISS DIANA?
MISS DIANA, MY FRIEND? COME WITH ME, ZACHARY. I'LL SHOW HIM NOW!
LET'S GO!!!
PUFF... I NEVER IMAGINED THAT BEING IN PRISON AND NOT MOVING WOULD MAKE MY LEGS SO STIFF.
CAN'T YOU MOVE ANY FASTER?
NO, AND IF WE GO ON LIKE THIS WE'LL NEVER CATCH HIM.
HOWEVER, JUDGING FROM WHAT I'VE SEEN, YOUR ARMS ARE STILL RATHER STRONG.
THAT'S TRUE. I WAS WORKING OUT BREAKING CHAINS.
PERFECT, THEN USE YOUR GREAT STRENGTH TO...

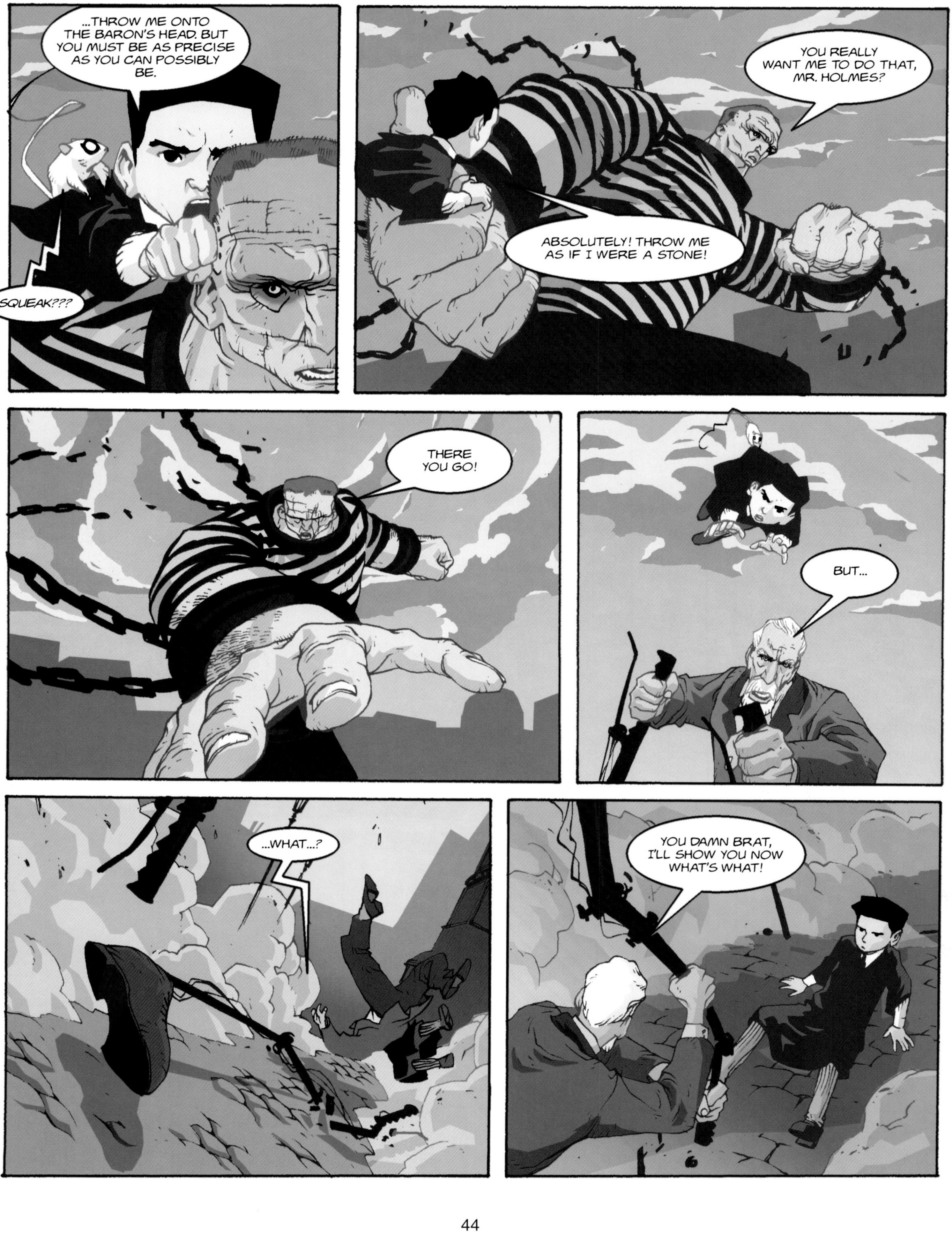
...THROW ME ONTO THE BARON'S HEAD. BUT YOU MUST BE AS PRECISE AS YOU CAN POSSIBLY BE.
SQUEAK???
YOU REALLY WANT ME TO DO THAT, MR. HOLMES?
ABSOLUTELY! THROW ME AS IF I WERE A STONE!
THERE YOU GO!
BUT...
...WHAT...?
YOU DAMN BRAT, I'LL SHOW YOU NOW WHAT'S WHAT!

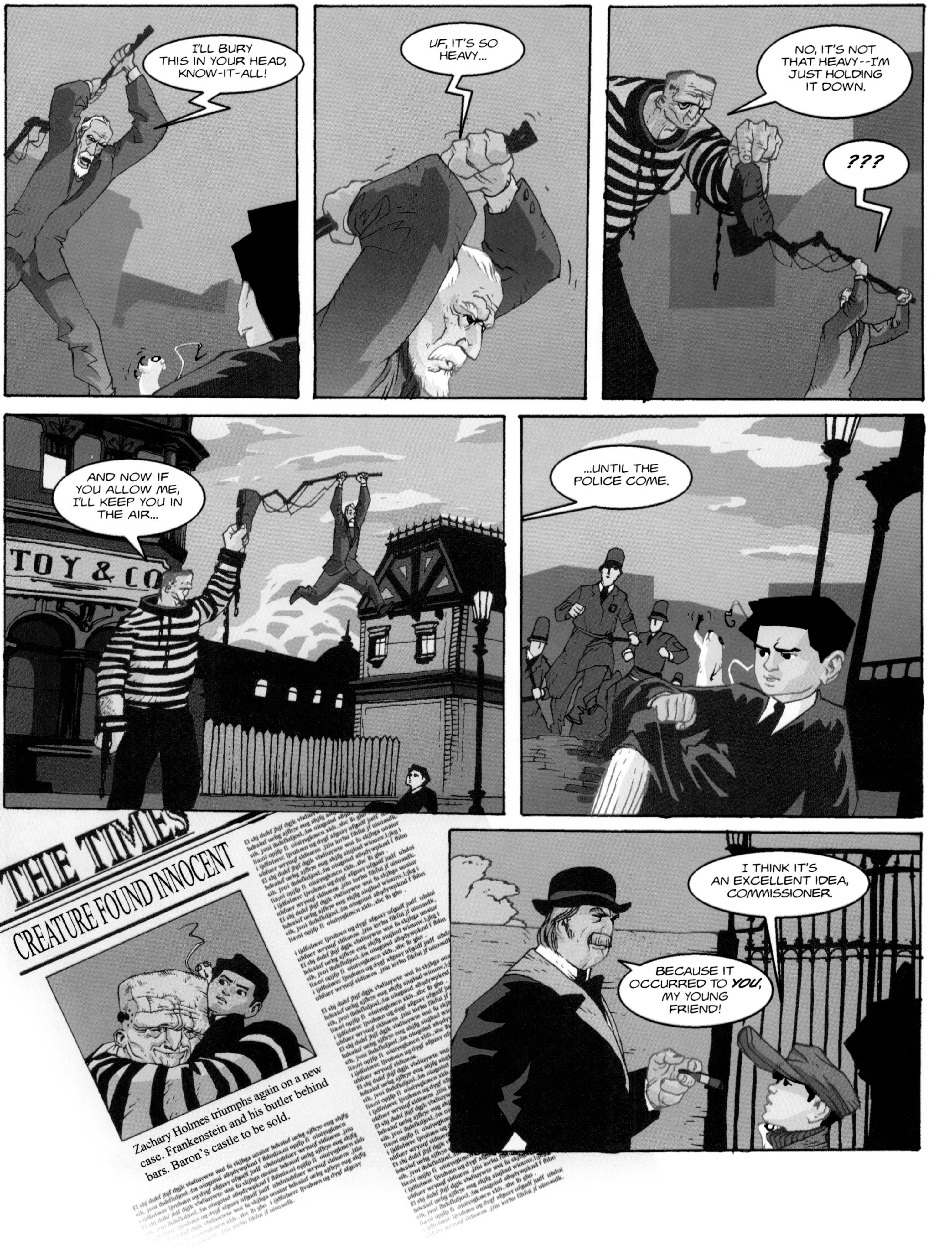
I'LL BURY THIS IN YOUR HEAD, KNOW-IT-ALL!
UF, IT'S SO HEAVY...
NO, IT'S NOT THAT HEAVY--I'M JUST HOLDING IT DOWN.
???
AND NOW IF YOU ALLOW ME, I'LL KEEP YOU IN THE AIR...
TOY & CO
...UNTIL THE POLICE COME.
THE TIMES
CREATURE FOUND INNOCENT
Zachary Holmes triumphs again on a new case. Frankenstein and his butler behind bars. Baron's castle to be sold.
I THINK IT'S AN EXCELLENT IDEA, COMMISSIONER.
BECAUSE IT OCCURRED TO *YOU*, MY YOUNG FRIEND!

BUT I'M ALSO CONVINCED THAT THE STREETS ARE GOING TO BE SAFER WITH...WITH *HIM* KEEPING ORDER.

I KNOW, HE'S TOO SENSIBLE TO MAKE A GOOD COP, BUT...

...I THINK HIS LOOKS WILL CONVINCE EVERYONE TO BEHAVE.

ZACHARY HOLMES...

...YOU'RE MY HERO. I WANTED TO TELL YOU THAT I ADMIRE YOUR COURAGE, INTELLIGENCE, AND WISDOM.

EXCUSE ME FOR BEING SO STRAIGHTFORWARD, BUT I'D LIKE TO BE YOUR FRIEND.

OH, DIANA, I'M SO GLAD TO HEAR THAT.

WHAT I WANTED MOST IN THE WORLD WAS TO BE YOUR FRIEND, BUT I WAS TOO SHY TO SAY IT ALOUD.

AND I LOVE TO DO IT BY YOUR SIDE.

SIGH. I LOVE TO STROLL ON THESE AUTUMN DAYS.

HA HA!

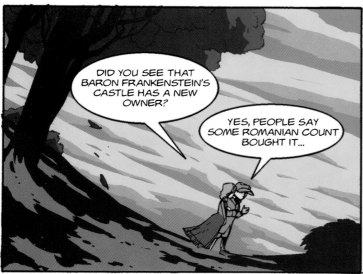

DID YOU SEE THAT BARON FRANKENSTEIN'S CASTLE HAS A NEW OWNER?

YES, PEOPLE SAY SOME ROMANIAN COUNT BOUGHT IT...

...*DRACULA* OR SOMETHING.

END OF BOOK #1

46

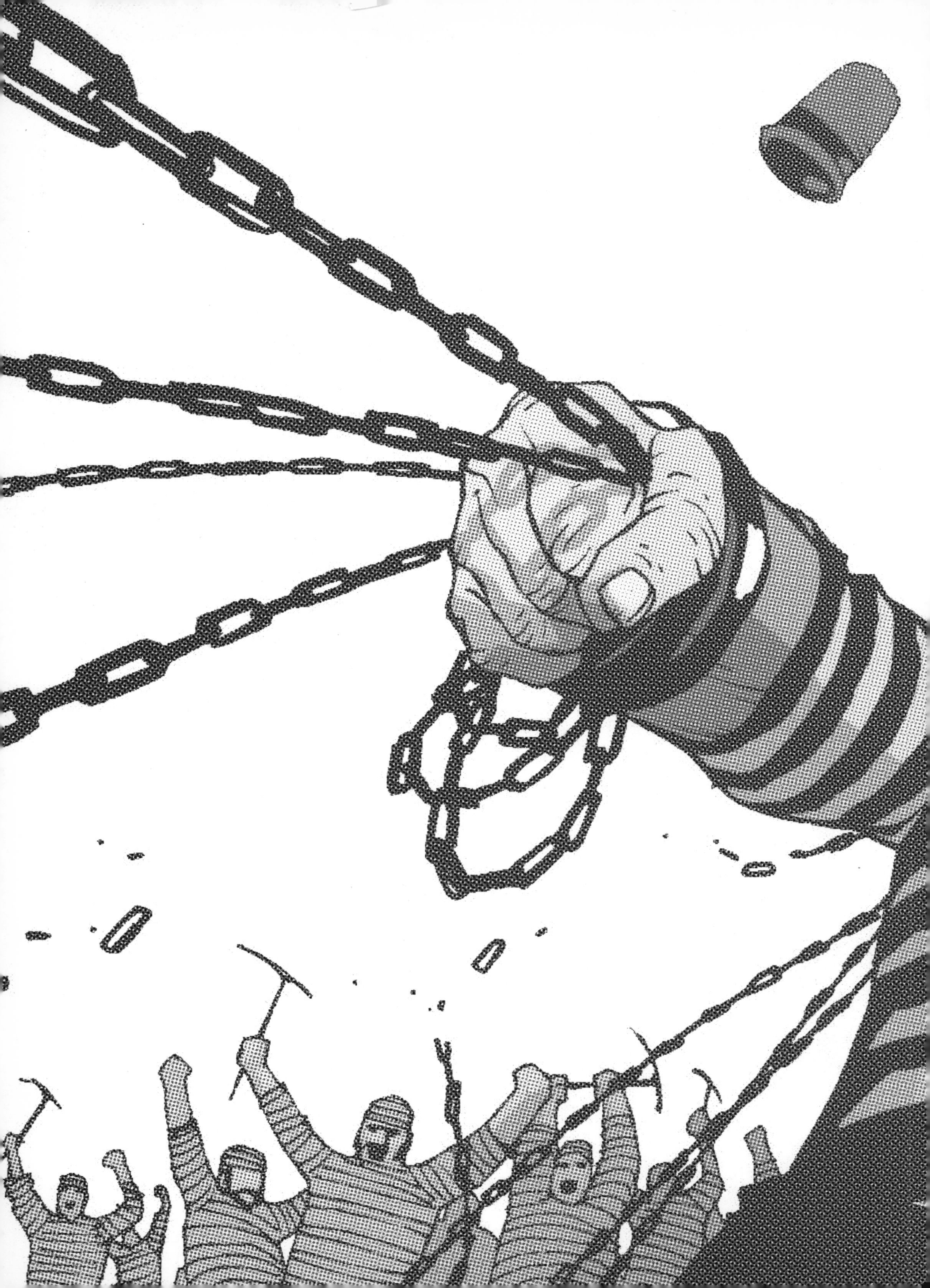